THE
CHRISTIAN
IN
MID-LIFE

THE CHRISTIAN IN
MID LIFE

1065

JERRY & MARY WHITE

NAVPRESS

A MINISTRY OF THE NAVIGATORS
P.O. Box 6000, Colorado Springs, CO 80934

The Navigators is an international, evangelical
Christian organization. Jesus Christ gave his
followers the Great Commission to go and
make disciples (Matthew 28:19). The aim of
The Navigators is to help fulfill that commission by multiplying laborers for Christ in every
nation.

NavPress is the publishing ministry of The
Navigators. NavPress publications are tools to
help Christians grow. Although publications
alone cannot make disciples or change lives,
they can help believers learn biblical discipleship, and apply what they learn to their lives
and ministries.

© 1980 by The Navigators
All rights reserved, including translation
Library of Congress Catalog Card Number:
80-83388
ISBN:0-89109-448-2
14480

Third printing, 1982

Printed in the United States of America

TO

Amy Knutson, Mary's late mother,
whose passage through mid-life
exemplified courage, perseverance,
and spiritual depth
while enduring failing health.
She lived above adversity,
and God's Spirit
triumphed through her.

Contents

Illustrations

Authors

Jerry White is the Pacific Regional Director for The Navigators in the United States.

He holds a Ph.D. in astronautics. During thirteen years with the United States Air Force, he served as a space mission controller at Cape Cannaveral and taught for six years at the U.S. Air Force Academy. He resigned from active duty in 1973, and is now a lieutenant colonel in the U.S. Air Force Reserve.

Mary Ann Knutson White attended Northwestern Bible College and the University of Washington. She holds a degree in English from the University of Colorado, and has worked as a secretary in government and industry.

The Whites' first contact with the Navigators was at the University of Washington. They also helped begin Navigator ministries at the Air Force Academy and Purdue. The Whites are currently involved in discipling ministries, speaking at seminars, and ministering in their local church.

Jerry and Mary are the authors of *Your Job: Survival or Satisfaction?* and *Friends and Friendship: The Secrets of Drawing Closer.* Jerry has also written *Honesty, Morality, and Conscience,* and *The Christian Student's How-to-Study Guide.*

Jerry and Mary live with their four children, Stephen, Katherine, Karen, and Kristin, near Seattle, Washington.

Preface

As we contemplated writing this book, Jerry mentioned the topic to his fifty-eight-year-old mother. He described middle age as thirty-five to fifty-five. She exclaimed, "That's not middle age! I'm middle aged!"

We delayed writing for a while, but the subject kept nagging us. Then daily crises hit and we seemed to be responding differently than we did in our thirties. We observed others experiencing similar difficulties. Finally we gave in to God's leading and began writing about coping with the puzzling changes of middle age.

Counseling, research, surveys, seminars, Bible studies, and personal experience form the basis of this book. It centers on biblical foundations. Its ideas are filtered through the viewpoints of both a man and a woman. It does not focus on an autobiographical catharsis of experience, but draws from the broad experiences of many people. We emphasize not simply survival, but how to effectively grow and minister in mid-life. We have attempted to make the book practical by including suggestions for solving problems, and for beginning and attaining personal growth throughout mid-life. Yet we have tried to avoid being simplistic and offering cookbook solutions.

We are indebted to many people who contributed to the study. The input from many who participated in our seminars at Pulpit Rock Church in Colorado Springs, Colorado, and at Our Saviour's Baptist Church in Federal Way, Washington, was extremely helpful as they detailed their mid-life experiences. We give special thanks to Judy Murray, Sharon Fox, and Glenda McFarlin for typing the manuscript.

This book can be used in classes or small groups with the accompanying Bible study, *A Bible Study on the Christian in Mid-life*. We pray that God will minister to your particular needs as you read and study.

Jerry and Mary White

CHAPTER 1

What Mid-life Crisis?

I was in a meeting when a proposal surfaced which included moving our family to another part of the country. My emotional response surprised me. I reacted in a way that I had not experienced before. I felt a sour mixture of fear, apprehension, negativism, turmoil, and guilt.

When I expressed this reaction strongly in the meeting, everyone was caught off guard since this was so uncharacteristic. I was usually calm, collected, and objective. Now I was emotional, scattered, and subjective. We delayed a decision for one month.

The next month was torturous for me internally. I struggled with my motives. Was I unavailable? I struggled with my reactions. Was I being unspiritual? I struggled with my anxiousness. Was I lacking in faith?

Now with 20/20 hindsight I can piece together some of the reasons for my reactions. The previous year had been stressful. I had accepted some new responsibility which included resolving several difficult personnel situations. My travel was heavy and each trip involved some difficult issues.

During that year I became acutely aware of my son's

impending departure from home upon graduation from high school. I realized the finality of my last chance to make a significant contribution to his life, and to some degree I felt I had failed in previous years. I felt I needed another year to solidify certain aspects of our relationship.

I knew I was using up my emotional and physical resources. In fact, I had already planned a period of recuperation. Then two unforeseen events interrupted my plans. Mary had to undergo major surgery. Then some complications extended her recovery time. Secondly, I had to face the possibility of a move. I was already tired and simply did not have the strength to easily absorb these two unexpected events.

Previously many people viewed me as a person of almost infinite capacity. Now I had to admit I could not handle something. I ran up the white flag of surrender. My pride was wounded. I had always been able to accept whatever was asked of me. I do not recall ever declining a direct request from my leadership. Now I experienced visions of failure and a diminishing career. I imagined people discussing that I had "peaked out in my ability," and was unavailable.

Without question, I had overextended myself. The major result was that my pride was dealt with severely. Subtle though it was, I had begun to believe what people said about my large capacity. Now I had to openly admit my dependence on God.

I turned forty in the middle of this experience. A new awareness drove me deeper into God's word and brought me to a fresh point of realism and surrender. In retrospect, I know the proposed move was not in God's plan, but my response was not necessarily the way to bring about his will. However, God used it to make me reassess my life and commitment.

Was it a mid-life crisis? Yes, I think so. A few years earlier or later might have evoked a drastically different response. Not only was I tired, but I was also living as though I were thirty instead of forty. My reserves and resiliency were less than before, but I had not recognized it.

This story may seem all too real to you, if you have encountered anything similar. Your experience may not have been as pronounced or immediate. Or you may not have experienced a mid-life crisis at all—but you will. Almost everyone does in varying degrees and intensities.

In fact, with all the attention given to mid-life crises and transitions, it becomes almost respectable to have one—if for no other reason than to relate to your friends! We joke about it. We notice our friends getting wrinkles and fat rolls. We comment woefully about our own. People in their twenties begin referring to us as "Mr." or "Mrs.", "sir" or "ma'am." We inwardly realize that a new era of life has begun with sometimes painful issues and crises.

Actually, we have no such thing as *a* mid-life crisis. Rather we have a series of crises—problems, successes, emotional traumas, and physical changes over a number of years. Different issues, different emotional responses, different times and intensities confront each person.

Your God-given uniqueness expresses itself even in the crises of life. No two people experience exactly the same thing, nor will a simple solution always work for two people with similar problems. But we can discover the common causes of these problems and find fundamental principles for solving them.

The very crisis engulfing you now can be the door to a more fulfilling and satisfying life than you imagined possible. It can also begin a deeper, more personal relationship with God. The change depends on how you face the issues and how you handle yourself at this key juncture of life.

In Chinese the character for the word crisis combines two other characters. One is the character for "danger" and the other is the character for "opportunity." So it is in mid-life—we encounter great dangers and equally great opportunities.

The danger lies in allowing the circumstances of mid-life to destroy your spiritual walk and emotional happiness. But the opportunity comes from deepening your life as you turn to God for strength and direction.

Crises Igniters

Just as lightning or a cigarette dropped in dry underbrush can ignite a raging forest fire, so every crisis is sparked by some incident or issue. The incident is not the cause, it only serves to ignite what was already there. We can identify many of the common problems that touch off a mid-life crisis.

Failure

Failure can affect us more in mid-life than at an earlier age. Failure at work, in marriage, or in life goals frquently sends people into depression. Advancing age reduces the possibilities for new starts and new successes.

Marriage Problems

Problems in marriage can become more acute as the years go by. We are less flexible and we expect more. Both partners lose their rose-colored glasses and take greater risks in conflict and directness. Lust and the temptation for extramarital affairs begin to exert an unusual pressure. As the children become older divorce seems more accepable. If there has been a previous marriage and this one is also going stale, hopelessness encroaches in a new way. A failure to develop a good marriage relationship during the early years of career-climbing begins to take its toll, leaving two strangers under the same roof.

Children

Only divorce or illness seem to drain as much emotional energy as dealing with the growth process of adolescent teens. And usually this happens in our mid-life at a time when we need to develop and change ourselves. Yet their demands are so immediate, and their crises and problems are so emotionally draining.

Another dilemma in mid-life is having another baby. This may send a thirty-eight-year-old mother into some depression and throw the father into confusion just when both thought they were reaching a stage of freedom.

Dead-end Careers

Finally realizing that our career dreams will not be realized can send us spiraling into a state of hopelessness. In our twenties, aspirations for the future motivate us. Optimism permeates our thinking. But by the mid-to-late thirties, experience allows us to look ahead to realistic end results for our career—and what we see may be far different from what we first hoped.

Health and Age

At some point we abruptly face the fact that youth with its physical vigor and stamina has gone. Shortness of breath, a lack of energy, and fat where we don't want it grimly remind us of our advancing age and changing health. Even when we reconcile the age issue in our minds, a major (or even minor) health problem gives us a glimpse of increasing frailty. With the onset of health problems, we may change from one who assumes good health is natural, to one who carefully guards health, emotions, and energy.

Typical Responses to Mid-life Crises

At the beginning of a four-week seminar on mid-life crises, we asked people to share their typical *feelings* and *responses* to a crisis. The group consisted of thirty-one men and women between the ages of thirty-five and fifty-seven. They were from varied backgrounds—married, single, and divorced. Here are some of their responses:

- Free-floating anxiety
- Frustration
- A lack of purpose or direction, even when purpose and direction had been obvious earlier
- Isolation. The sense of being alone with no one who cares or can help
- A changed self-concept: sudden shifts in my view of my ambition and potential
- Feelings of worthlessness: The suspicion that I no longer have a contribution to make and my usefulness has ended
- Feelings of being trapped: the claustrophobia of life when I think there is no way out—either at work or in marriage
- Lust: a new tendency to consider mental and physical infidelity
- A declining sexual drive for no apparent reason
- Fear about financial matters that never bothered me before
- Realizing the universality of growing older and its ac-

companying lack of health, stamina, and oppor-
tunities
- Weariness and fatigue: a sense of constantly being
tired, but not from obvious age or health problems
- Self-centered sympathy: feeling I'm getting a "raw
deal" or that people don't understand me
- Rebellion in areas I once accepted calmly
- Giving up: an overwhelming temptation to quit a
task, a job, a project, or a marriage
- Depression: an empty, unexplainable feeling of being
down emotionally
- Boredom with things that once were stimulating
- Anger over issues and incidents I once tolerated
- Bitterness: an anger against people or situations
- Hopelessness: the feeling that no matter what I do the
situation will not improve
- Easily surfaced emotions: crying with little provocation
- Feeling I will "explode": the internal pressure that
makes me feel I am about to have a nervous break-
down

This is a grim list. Just reading it makes us feel
depressed. Yet, this list reflects reality for many people,
Christian and non-Christian. The intensity of these feelings far exceeds the same feelings at other ages. These feelings are real, laced with a depth of hurt rarely expressed to
others. They usually smolder and ferment until they boil
over with a damaging blow to marriage, health, or career.

These feelings are complex, caused by no single incident or background; consequently the feelings can't be
changed by simple answers. But there are roots and
reasons—and answers. Definite help can be found in the
Scriptures and in a personal relationship with Jesus Christ.
He is Lord over our feelings as well as our circumstances.

Transition and Change

We have rarely been in a discussion about these issues without someone asking, "What age is middle age?" We hear sayings like, "You're as old as you feel and as young as you think," or "Age is a matter of the mind," or "Dress young and you'll act young." But no matter how encouraging the quote, it will not make us *be* younger. Age creeps upon us with no possibility of reversal or slowing down. We cannot turn back the clock, even for a second.

Age is change—small changes, large changes, slow changes, imperceptible changes—but always change. Learning to live with change and transition is a major issue in coping with mid-life.

In one sense, all of life is a transition from one age to another. Over time the changes are distinct enough that we can classify life into general age categories, as in this arrangement:

Childhood	0-12
Adolescence	13-20
Young Adult	21-35
Mid-life	35-55
Mature Adulthood	55-70
Elderly	70 and older

Daniel Levinson uses slightly different age boundaries but further defines certain year groups as "transition." He calls seventeen to twenty-two the early adult transition, forty to forty-five the mid-life transition, fifty to fifty-five the age fifty transition and sixty to sixty-five the late adult transition.

Our concern here is the mid-life area, and, consequently, the mid-life transition. We would suggest that this transition can occur as early as age thirty or as late as sixty for different individuals.

In addition to age there is another key indicator of mid-life—*events*. Certain events provide transitions in life which stimulate emotional responses just as strongly as does age. These events are often the "firsts" of our lives—marriage, job, divorce, and child. A typical sequence would be:

High school to college (or job)
College (or high school) to job
Job change
Marriage
Children
Divorce (Divorce is so common that it must now be included, though it is not right.)
Teenage children
Career change
Illness
The "empty nest"
Menopause
Retirement

All these transitions evoke emotional responses and drains. But when do these events generally occur? Look at Figure 1-1.

Notice the tremendous concentration of emotionally draining events frequently occurring in mid-life. Do you still wonder why stress and problems appear in mid-life? Just at the time when sinking roots and settling down begins to seem attractive, compelling changes invade and overturn our plans.

Although we define mid-life as ages thirty-five to fifty-five, understand that some of the changes and events which characterize mid-life may occur as early as thirty or as late as sixty. Usually, however, the years from forty to fifty are the most stressful and eventful.

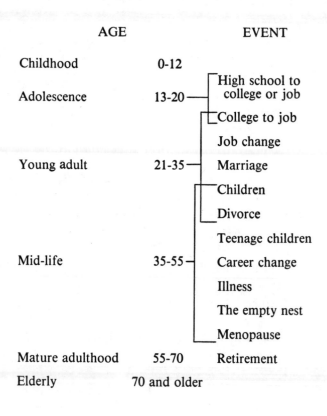

AGE		EVENT
Childhood	0-12	
Adolescence	13-20	High school to college or job
		College to job
		Job change
Young adult	21-35	Marriage
		Children
		Divorce
		Teenage children
Mid-life	35-55	Career change
		Illness
		The empty nest
		Menopause
Mature adulthood	55-70	Retirement
Elderly	70 and older	

Figure 1-1

Every change—a new job, a move, a child leaving home, being fired, or a divorce—has the potential of setting off a crisis and signaling our entrance to mid-life.

But, as we will see, crises can be avoided—and especially shortened. Our tolerance for change can be developed by learning to be more flexible. If we resist change in our twenties, how can we ever expect anything other than rigidity and inflexibility in our thirties and forties? Change is the spice of life or the strife of life—depending on your viewpoint. Welcomed, it serves and develops. Feared and resisted, it petrifies and shatters.

Mid-life for Christians

Should mid-life be different for Christians? Yes. Is mid-life automatically different for Christians? No. Do most Christians handle mid-life problems better than non-Christians? Unfortunately, no. Being a Christian is purported to make us happier and to solve our problems. But this doesn't seem true for so many.

The reason? Many people *are* Christians but they do not apply Christian truth and practice to their lives. They think, live, and act like non-Christians and so they reap the same results. But Christians do have resources which are unavailable to non-Christians, if they will but use them.

"They will still bear fruit in old age, they will stay fresh and green" (Psalm 92:14). This verse reflects the desire of every Christian. We do not want to simply survive mid-life. We want to engage triumphantly in a life of new fruitfulness and increased usefulness to God.

Consider these fundamental resources a Christian has that a non-Christian does not:

1. The Christian possesses eternal life (see John 5:25). This eternal life is not only a future experience

beyond death. It begins now for all of life. Many people simply "assume" they are Christian because for the most part they are church attenders or members, or because they live a moral, upright life. But that is not what makes a person a Christian. We become acutely aware of our need for God as we encounter problems beyond our control. We may pray and go to church more regularly, but discover that our prayers are bouncing off the ceiling.

This may be the time to make sure you have actually understood the gospel and become a true Christian. The first step in becoming a Christian is to realize and admit you have sinned and have no hope of eternal life unless this sin is forgiven. "For all have sinned and fall short of the glory of God" (Romans 3:23). The results of this sin are described in Romans 6:23—"For the wages of sin is death, but the gift of God is eternal life in Christ Jesus our Lord." Even though we have sinned, God provided a way to eternal life through Jesus Christ.

But what did Christ do to rescue us from the penalty of sin? He died on a cross in our place to make eternal life possible. He was our substitute. He could do this because he was the Son of God and was sinless. "But God demonstrates his own love for us in this: While we were still sinners, Christ died for us." (Romans 5:8). The cardinal facts about Christ are that he was the Son of God, he died for man's sin, and he rose again from the dead.

Though all this is true, it is not effective for us unless we respond in the right way to what Christ offers. How do you make it effective for yourself? You simply need to believe in Christ—to accept him as your personal Savior, admitting your need.

Now, many believe intellectually in Christ in
much the same way they believe in Abraham Lincoln.
The difference is in believing and accepting by faith
that Christ was who he said he was, and that he
forgives your sin and gives you eternal life. "For God
so loved the world, that he gave his one and only
Son, that whoever believes in him shall not perish but
have eternal life" (John 3:16). "He who believes in
the Son has eternal life; but he who does not obey the
Son shall not see life, but the wrath of God abides on
him" (John 3:36).

This eternal life comes by asking Jesus Christ to
be one's Savior and Lord—a conscious decision based
on the facts of Scripture. By this step of faith a person acknowledges that *only* through Christ's deity,
death, and resurrection can one become a Christian
and have eternal life. This is no trivial matter. If how
to become a Christian is not clear to you, we suggest
further study of the Bible, especially in the Gospel of
John. Personal salvation establishes the foundation
for dealing with every crisis of life.[2]

2. The Christian possesses the Holy Spirit. Jesus said, "I
   will ask the Father, and he will give you another
   Counselor to be with you forever—the Spirit of
   truth," (John 14:16-17). This Counselor is the Holy
   Spirit. He is the empowering force in our lives. When
   we fall into difficult circumstances the Holy Spirit
   gives us power to endure. He gives enlightenment as
   we read the Scriptures and guidance on how to live.
   "But when he, the Spirit of truth, comes, he will
   guide you into all truth" (John 16:13).

   Non-Christians have no access to this inner
   spiritual power. They must depend only on their own
   minds and wills to face life. Regrettably, many Chris-

tians do not take advantage of the power available to them, but rather rely on non-Christian ways of living and thinking.

Christians should claim promises like 2 Peter 1:3: "His divine power has given us everything we need for life and godliness through our knowledge of him who called us by his own glory and goodness." God has provided power for every situation—real power, not just a mystical fantasy or theory. The key to tapping God's power is obedience. Obey God's word. Apply its principles to your life today.

3. The Christian possesses the word of God, the Bible. "All Scripture is inspired by God and profitable for teaching, for reproof, for correction, for training in righteousness" (2 Timothy 3:16). The Bible contains the answer for every problem a person faces. But doesn't a non-Christian have the same resource? Only in a limited sense. A non-Christian can apply the principles of the Bible, but it will not have the power since the Scriptures have never been activated by receiving Christ. The word of God is a never-ending reserve for guidance and direction but a closed Bible cannot help. We must delve into it, search out its depths and apply it to our lives. In mid-life, answers are not simply a cookbook recipe, nor is the Bible simply an answer book. Through the illuminating power of the Holy Spirit we can discover truth that will revolutionize our lives.

Objectives of this Book

The objectives of this book are direct and specific:

1. Identify the major *problems* of mid-life.
2. Isolate basic *causes* of the problems. One cause may manifest itself in many forms of surface problems.
3. Help people in mid-life *understand* what they are encountering. Being forewarned is being forearmed. If we can be aware of what might happen to us, we will have less anxiety when it happens. We don't want to create a fatalistic attitude or an expectant dread. We realize that much of what is discussed may never happen to you. But it is our hope that many possible problems will be avoided because you will have learned how to recognize them.
4. Find biblical guidelines for *solving* the problems and alleviating the causes. Our purpose is to present practical, biblical help for real issues. We want to develop a perspective to help you see where mid-life issues fit in the totality of life. We want to counsel from a spiritual basis, not a worldly base, and to help in a *spiritual* and a *practical* manner, not just theoretically. Finally, we want to isolate issues that are primarily physical in nature and can be treated medically, or which are a normal part of growing older.
5. Discover and emphasize the *positive* aspects of mid-life and *learn* how to capitalize on them. We want to equip you to launch into life with greater potential and fulfillment.

   One word of encouragement. Few people, very few, make their major contribution in life before mid-life. Mid-life gives us the opportunity to live to the fullest and to serve others more effectively than at any other time in life.
6. Create an open, honest, *sharing* environment. We can take comfort in knowing that others are experiencing the same things. Don't suffer silently and

alone. Seek out others for mutual help and encouragement.

This book is meant to be shared, discussed, argued with and added to. The therapy of talking and sharing is invaluable. This book is not complete. It does not cover every experience, problem, or need. But it does lay a foundation for growth and development as you navigate the waters of mid-life.

All of these objectives will be of little personal value to you unless you are open and honest—with yourself, your spouse, and some select friends. And, most importantly, there will be no solution without God's direct guidance and help. Stop right now and ask God to work in your life as you read the remaining chapters. Ask him to give you a new lease on life—physically, emotionally, and spiritually.

Mid-life will be either a great adventure or a great trial. It's your choice.

NOTES: 1. Daniel J. Levinson, *The Seasons of a Man's Life* (New York: Alfred A. Knopf, Inc., 1978), page 57.

2. For further information we recommend: *How to Be Born Again*, by Billy Graham (Waco, Texas: Word Books, 1977), and *Basic Christianity*, by John R. W. Stott (Grand Rapids, Michigan: William B. Eerdmans Publishing Company, 1974).

CHAPTER 2

Women in Mid-life

During a routine checkup my gynecologist discovered I had an ovarian cyst. He didn't seem greatly concerned and prescribed medicinal treatment for a month to see how the cyst would react.

"Any woman over forty must be cautious," he said.

During that month I rarely thought about the cyst, praying occasionally that the treatment would be effective and expecting the cyst to disappear. But when I was reexamined, it was still there and no smaller. The doctor immediately suggested exploratory surgery. We had planned to leave soon on a ten-day speaking trip, so he encouraged us to go ahead with our plans, but schedule surgery as soon as we returned.

"The chances of malignancy are slight, but we need to find out," the doctor told me. "If you were twenty-five, thirty, or even thirty-five, we wouldn't be quite so concerned." There it was: the specter of mid-life—the physical reality of aging—influencing the doctor's approach to my health.

After summoning the prayers of many friends, we took the trip with a sense of God's presence and grace. We prayed that our concern about the surgery and all its accompanying "what ifs" would not distract us from ministering to others.

But there were times when we reviewed the possibilities: What if I had a long hospital stay and a difficult recovery? What if the cyst were cancerous? Could it be cured? What if Jerry couldn't manage his work and the family if I was ill?

The unknowns of life assume greater proportions in our middle years. The fresh opportunities of youth have gone, and we are more aware of life's brevity. If things don't follow our plans, or take a sudden negative turn, we panic.

The only answer to the "what ifs" of life is daily trust in the sovereignty and goodness of God. "In all things God works for the good of those who love him, who have been called according to his purpose" (Romans 8:28). He says, "My grace is sufficient for you, for my power is made perfect in weakness" (2 Corinthians 12:9). Such truths become a reality in our lives when we practice and experience them. The Apostle Paul wrote those words after experiencing personal hardships and encountering unexpected events frequently for many years. He had found that only God could quiet his emotions and give him confidence for the future.

After returning from our trip, I saw the doctor for a pre-surgery checkup, and he determined that the cyst had shrunk considerably and surgery was unnecessary. Whew! Praise God!

In that instance we were spared. But God could choose at any time to allow us to experience a physical illness, the death of a family member, a problem with our children, some financial loss, or any one of a number of hardships or personal failures. We need to keep alert, spiritually prepared, and emotionally stable, so we can accept these crises with grace, courage, and confidence in God.

Crisis Indicators

With some idea of possible transitions or problems to expect in their middle years, women can more readily prepare to meet them with a godly perspective. These times can be an invaluable opportunity for God to draw them into a sweeter relationship with himself and to mold their characters into the image of Jesus Christ.

Appearance

What can be more startling to a woman of forty than to unexpectedly see her relaxed reflection in a mirror? Her jumbled thoughts ask, "Does my stomach really sag? Why does my hair look so dull? Why had I never noticed the deep wrinkles around my mouth? Is that a double chin as well?"

We see what we want to see. We may notice wrinkles around our eyes, but that isn't so bad because the jaw line is still firm. What if the waistline is a little thick? Just standing a little straighter camouflages that.

In mid-life many women rationalize, ignore, or resent the changes in their appearance rather than accepting them as one of the marks of God's gift of years. If you are skeptical about the changes in your once youthful appearance, attend a class reunion. Women you haven't seen for ten or twenty years will look distinctly older—wrinkled, heavy, sagging, and gray. A few will still retain their smooth skin and firm figures, but they have probably done so with considerable effort and expense.

Our society places an inordinate emphasis on physical attractiveness. As Dr. James Dobson says, "Without question, the most highly valued personal attribute in our culture (and most others) is physical attractiveness."[1] Any woman who varies from the ideal of beauty automatically loses esteem among her peers.

We should have outgrown such standards by our middle years, but unfortunately we haven't. Retailers cater as much to the middle-aged as to the young. We see stores with well-stocked cosmetic counters, numerous exercise clubs, cosmetic surgeons (almost three dozen in our city alone), bulging clothes racks in fashionably stocked stores, and dozens of magazines devoted to beautifying the human body.

Advertisers want women to believe they will be disliked and shunned if they have a few flakes of dandruff on the collar, one tiny liver spot on the hand, a wrinkle in their panty hose, or any trace of a wrinkle or blemish. We know, at least intellectually, that "the Lord looks at the heart" but the fact that "man looks at the outward appearance" (1 Samuel 16:7) colors our thinking.

Christian women seek to beautify themselves just as others do. And Christian women do have a responsibility to appear as attractive and as well-groomed as time and finances permit. But they also need the spiritual and personal maturity to accept the aging process as a natural, and yes, a welcome indication of life's progression. This also means accepting others' imperfections as well.

While our family was attending a horseback-riding performance at a state fair, a severely handicapped young man was brought in his wheelchair and placed near the entrance to the grandstand. He was confined to his chair. His hands and face moved with involuntary twitches continuously. But from his clear expression and the interested way he observed the performance, we sensed that he was an intelligent young man.

Many people streamed by him as they were entering or leaving the stadium. After one quick look at the young man they would glance away and hurry by. Finally another young man came by, wearing broken sandles, torn jeans, and a rumpled shirt, his long hair bound with a rubber band. But he alone stopped, smiled, looked directly at the young man and said, "Hey, how are you today?" before walking on. Although he was careless about his own appearance, he more than all the others who passed by showed that he recognized the worth of the young man in the wheelchair.

A friend of ours recently described a conversation she had with a young couple, Joe and Kathy. Joe frequently made suggestions to Kathy about her hairstyle, clothing, and posture, and often criticized her general appearance. After listening to his stream of criticism, our friend suggested to Joe that he consider the impression he was conveying to his wife. All of his comments focused on her external appearance and not on her inner person.

"What will Kathy do in the years to come when she knows her physical attractiveness is diminishing?" our friend asked. "What will she do when her skin wrinkles and sags? What if she loses a breast to a mastectomy? Or what if her hair turns prematurely gray? She can only assume that your approval and affection will be withdrawn because she has heard only your comments about her physical appearance." Joe accepted the suggestions and began eliminating his criticisms and learning to see his wife as a complete person.

Our appearance will change. No one can nullify the effects of aging. But our response to these changes will determine our inner serenity and self-acceptance.

Health

Shirley is a good friend. After years of serving the Lord on the mission field and caring for her own children and husband, she was stricken with several illnesses in mid-life. She had diabetes, then cancer, and finally heart surgery. All were disabling, limiting, difficult illnesses. Her failing health has affected her appearance, her capacity as a wife, mother and homemaker, and her service in her community and church. Yet she cannot change her history and must trust God for the grace to endure.

As we see godly women like Shirley who suffer illness, we develop a greater appreciation for our own health. We realize how fragile our bodies really are, and that our good health may deteriorate at any time.

Generally, young women as well as men feel invincible physically. They are strong, healthy, and energetic. But as they grow older, their bodies begin to change and break down in several ways.

Menopause begins with varying symptoms—annoying hot flashes, days of depression, and unpredictable menstrual periods. Some women encounter instant menopause due to surgery. Either way, it is an inevitable indication of a changing body in mid-life.

Diminishing energy also affects women. One mother of teens said, "I cared for a toddler for three days and almost went crazy. I just don't have the energy anymore to take care of little children." A woman of forty can't handle either the variety or the intensity of physical labor that she could at twenty. She can't push the vacuum as fast as she once did, she now drives to the car wash instead of scrubbing the car herself, and preparing a dinner party tires her more than it once did.

Because her energy begins to flag, she must wisely select activities and plan her time to conserve energy for important tasks.

Physical limitations of several kinds gradually become apparent: faltering vision and hearing, maybe a little tremor in the hands, or arthritic twinges on rainy mornings. Bunions, aching knees, and sore backs all remind us of our limitations. Perhaps you and a friend used to have a weekly tennis date, but now you lunch together. Window shopping used to be great fun, but now your feet begin to hurt after an hour of walking. These changes may be resented, but they come just the same and tell us our bodies are deteriorating.

Women as well as men often fear *serious illness* in mid-life, knowing their new vulnerability. Illnesses last longer and recovery is slower. It is a natural response to worry that symptoms may suggest a dread disease and fear the consequences, though knowing God is in control.

But women need not be defeated by sickness when it comes. My mother developed a serious degenerative illness in mid-life and it progressed for several years until her death in her late fifties. The disease gradually reduced her from an able, gifted woman to one who was completely bedridden.

But with the deterioration of her health, a spiritual strength emerged that may never have flourished if God had not limited her physically. She completely accepted the changes and adapted to the circumstances in which God placed her. After a day in bed she once told her husband, "The days pass so quickly. There are so many people to pray for."

If the Lord chooses to allow illness, he also gives us the grace and comfort to accept and adapt. "God is able to make all grace abound to you, so that in all things at all times, having all that you need, you will abound in every good work" (2 Corinthians 8:7).

Loneliness

One woman said recently: "I feel so alone. I have a lovely home, a faithful husband, an active social life, but I don't know of one person who is really interested in me—what I think, what matters to me, and who I am inside. I feel like I'm living alone, suspended in time, while everyone around me goes on with the business of living."

During their middle years many women experience a deep sense of loneliness and isolation. Their children are either active teens or have left home, and their husbands are concentrating on careers. An emphasis on liberation, a proper self-image, fulfillment, and a rewarding career all combine to confuse and isolate the middle-aged woman. Changing social values further complicate these issues. How does a woman discover what will bring her satisfaction and fulfillment? In an attempt to ignore or mask their loneliness, many develop attitudes of indifference, hostility, or even frivolity and self-indulgence.

Jane, the wife of a successful executive, raised three daughters and kept a lovely home. She was well-known in the community for her activities. But when her daughters left home, she felt empty and lonely. She discovered that although she loved her husband as he loved her, they had allowed years to pass while she concentrated on the children and he majored on his career. They were nominally Christian, preferring to give money to the Lord's work rather than being personally involved.

Jane's sister, Joyce, observed Jane's lonely frustration. Joyce knew God intimately and realized Jane needed a fresh approach to spiritual things. She encouraged Jane to read the Scriptures and pray daily. She then urged her sister to take an interest in other people.

Jane's interests changed as she developed consistent communication with God. She volunteered to teach a girls'

Sunday school class—something she had not done since she was in college. She began to love these girls and eagerly anticipated each Sunday with them. She visited them in their homes and even led one girl's mother to Christ.

About a year after Joyce had first talked to her, Jane suddenly realized, "Why, I haven't thought about being lonely for months. Thank you, Lord. And thank you, Joyce."

Anxiety

Many women are apprehensive and uneasy when they face new developments in mid-life. Their anxiety may develop over many years, but it can explode suddenly with devastating results.

A woman may be anxious about her children and the possible harm, spiritual and physical, which they might encounter. Or she may be worried about finances, her husband's interest in her, her aging parents' health and welfare, her own health, problems in her church, the state of the world—anything and everything, both known and unknown.

Anxiety interferes with a woman's relationships and makes it difficult to accomplish tasks, and to plan and schedule. Somehow her mind refuses to concentrate on anything except possible problems.

Someone has said that 90 percent of the things we worry about never happen. If this is true, we waste much of our physical and emotional energy by allowing anxiety to sap our strength, raise our blood pressure, increase our pulse rate, and tense our muscles.

An anxious woman fills her mind with self-doubt and fear. She dreads responsibility and making decisions, and, most of all, she dreads her feeling of anxiety.

God has provided communication with himself as the

antidote for anxiety, as Paul wrote in Philippians 4:6—
"Do not be anxious about anything, but in everything, by
prayer and petition, with thanksgiving, present your requests to God."

Practicing this command to pray requires discipline of
the mind and soul—a willingness and readiness to take all
our troubles and worries into the presence of God and then
concentrate on thanksgiving. The result—inward peace
that is unavailable from any other source—protects the
mind from renewed attacks of anxiety.

Anger

We can list several issues in mid-life which can
stimulate anger in women:

- Lack of appreciation or approval at home or at work
- Feeling personally unfulfilled
- No career outside the home
- Unused gifts and talents
- The need to work to provide extra income
- Rebellious children
- Personal failure
- Undeveloped talent
- Full schedules
- Unreasonable demands from family and friends

Some women feel mid-life ends their opportunities for
growth and development in their education, career, or personal ministry, and they become angry and bitter. Many
feel that mid-life presents a last chance to change their
life's direction and to reach out once more for their goals
and dreams. If those changes don't come, they seethe with
inward resentment that bursts into outward actions
ultimately.

Anger manifests itself in many ways:

- Lack of love
- Aggressiveness
- A critical spirit
- Malicious speech
- Deep, inner bitterness
- Hatred
- Spiritual coldness

When we reach mid-life we need to develop the maturity to recognize anger for what it is—sin—and to confess it and avoid it in the future.

Ultimately all anger is directed toward God because we think he allowed certain events but not others, and therefore didn't arrange things to suit us.

Anger is a dangerous, destructive emotion, both internally and toward others. David wrote in Psalm 37:8, "Refrain from anger and turn from wrath; do not fret—it leads only to evil." Paul knew of the devastating results of anger when he wrote in Colossians 3:8, "But now you must rid yourselves of all such things as these: anger, rage, malice, slander and filthy language from your lips."

Powerlessness

Life seemed more controllable when we were younger. If something negative happened, we felt we had plenty of time to recover. In mid-life, however, we feel control slipping away. Irreversible events take place—parents die, our health fails, our children may marry someone we think is the wrong person, we suffer through a divorce, or we are fired from a job.

Then we panic because we feel there is little hope of restoring our former happiness. The years are slipping away and we can't force events to meet our expectations. We struggle and manipulate but still seem powerless to change the course of our lives.

I met to a woman who seemed locked into impossible circumstances. Her husband, a pastor, left her for another woman. Her children had left home, her income was meager, and her health was beginning to crumble. Her husband would not return, the children must make their own lives, and her limited training prevented her from changing jobs. She could not keep the pressure from draining her health and stamina.

From time to time we all feel caught in the grip of circumstances or under the control of others. Only a firm conviction that God controls everything can give stability and meaning to such difficult situations.

Spiritual Emptiness

Matthew and Sandy had been married for twenty-three years. During that time they were active in their church and the spiritual life of their community. Suddenly Matthew announced he was going to divorce Sandy, move to another state, build a small cabin in the mountains, and pursue a writing career. Sandy listened in stunned silence. Matthew's abrupt rejection and unwillingness to consider her pleading for a reconciliation devastated Sandy. For a short time she sought consolation among church friends but found they were awkward and uncomfortable in her presence. In bitter frustration she stopped attending church. She began dating non-Christian men and soon drifted into an unhappy life of sin.

Was Matthew to blame? Partly. But although Sandy had devoted years of her life to Christian "activities" she had neglected her own spiritual growth and when trials came, she collapsed. She was a spiritual baby.

It's overwhelming to realize that after years of professing to be a Christian our spiritual exercises can become routine and meaningless, or to see that our growth has been minimal. In what should be a time for helping others we have nothing to give. All we know are dry spells of spiritual indifference and drifting from the things of God.

In churches all across America, women faithfully attend services and participate in women's Bible studies and prayer groups. But often it's only a public performance. Their private walk with God does not match their public display. Certainly they receive blessing and enrichment from the group activities, but all the while they are missing God's very best. If you have reached mid-life and realize your lack of spiritual depth, don't be discouraged. Be grateful God has given you the insight to recognize your failure. Resolve to begin growing as a disciple of Christ.

Career Problems

Mid-life presents a time of upheaval in many women's careers. Because they gain greater personal freedom as their children leave home, many women seek a new or more challenging career. Many experience growing disillusionment with the rewards of housework and feel an increasing restlessness, a desire for something more. They would like to expand their capacities, capabilities, and income.

This is a sensitive area for a married woman because her career involves the entire family. Taking a job for the first time or accepting another job with increased responsibilities will reduce the time a woman can give at home. She may meet with resentment from her family. She will need to learn to cope with additional pressures. But possible problems should not deter a woman who feels that God is leading her to work.

Part-time jobs offer an excellent alternative to full-time housework. Career training is readily available. But anyone who looks for life's fulfillment in a career alone makes a serious mistake. Jobs can be interesting, stimulating, and rewarding; but true fulfillment comes only through a relationship with God and by making a contribution to other people's lives.

Family Struggles

Many factors disturb marriage during mid-life—growing apart, diverging interests and goals, divorce, declining sexual drive, unfaithfulness, the excessive pursuit of career goals, and disagreement over relationships with children.

Children, too, give us many reasons for concern. They fail to meet our expectations, they rebel openly against us and God, they disappoint and embarrass us with their lifestyle. One mother said of her married daughter and husband, "They are so touchy. We see many things wrong in their home, but we don't say a word because we would lose them. We just pray."

During the middle years family relationships should be one of the strongest and most sustaining aspects of life. But difficulties creep in and destroy that support. Yet it is never too late to restore broken relationships. We need to pay great attention in our middle years to family interaction and the strengthening of family bonds.

Coming Out Ahead

The signs of trouble are many. But there are definite actions women can take to prevent mid-life problems from becoming overwhelming.

Maintain a Strong Spiritual Focus

A few years ago I had lunch with Mattie, a Christian woman. The conversation turned to spiritual matters. I asked Mattie how her relationship with the Lord was progressing.

"Oh, fine, fine," Mattie answered, "I've been in church almost every Sunday this year."

"What about personal Bible reading and prayer?" I asked. "Church attendance is very important but it cannot replace reading the Bible daily, thinking and meditating on what you've read, and then praying. Do you do that now?"

"Well, no, not exactly. Sometimes I read the Scripture portion assigned with the Sunday school lesson, but, honestly, I'm so busy now. Each day is crammed full and I don't know how I could add something like that. Doesn't it take a lot of time?"

"It takes as much time as you will give it. But Mattie, you will find that Bible reading and prayer are more important than breakfast, brushing your teeth, or going to work. Once you've experienced God speaking to you personally from his word, you won't want to miss that. Sermons and Sunday school lessons are excellent, but they can't substitute for the time you spend alone with God. Why don't you try it this week for seven minutes each day?" I gave her the booklet entitled "Seven Minutes with God."[2]

About a week later we met again. Mattie enthusiastically related how she was following the suggestions for a seven-minute daily program and felt that every minute was well spent. She planned to increase her time to ten minutes daily. Now, three years later, she spends thirty to forty minutes daily praying, reading her Bible, and thinking over the things she has read.

When I first talked with her and suggested she seek

God on a personal level, Mattie had experienced several crises in her life. Her teenage daughter had left home twice and both times was apprehended by the police for public drunkenness. Mattie had been laid off from her executive secretarial job when the company she worked for folded. At the time those circumstances were difficult to live with, but after having personal devotions for a year her life changed. Some problems remained, but her attitude was completely different.

She began to understand and experience, as we all must, that God is sovereign and he allows all of the events in our lives. His timing for circumstances cannot be challenged because he knows them all and permits them. As C.W. Welch has paraphrased Romans 8:28:

> The Lord may not have planned that this should overtake me, but he has most certainly permitted it. Therefore though it were an attack of an enemy, by the time it reaches me, it has the Lord's permission, and therefore all is well. He will make it work, together with all life's experiences, for good.

To accept God's sovereignty we must trust him, and to trust him we must know him. The best way to know him is to learn about him (and about us) in his word, the Bible.

A woman develops trust in her husband by personal observation and experience. She does not rely on someone else to tell her what he is like or why she should trust him. Rather, she lives with him day by day, she observes him, she talks with him, and personally learns to trust him.

The same is true in our walk with God. If we spend some time every day learning to know him through the Scriptures, we quickly develop a new perspective on his will and his goodness to us.

Not long ago I spoke with a woman who was desperate for God's presence in her life. She said, "I feel so spiritually dry. I feel like a fake. I know I'm a Christian because I personally accepted Christ as my Savior and have an assurance of eternal life. But I just feel empty."

When I urged her to take some time each day to read Scripture, pray, and study, she answered, "Well, I know you feel that's the answer, but you have no idea how busy I am. There's nothing I could cut from my schedule." As far as I know, she is still frustrated and spiritually empty.

Someone has said that God does not reveal himself to the curious but to the dedicated. In our middle years we want to be more than curious onlookers at the spiritual feast God has for us. We want to be dedicated participants.

Stay Healthy

Our physical bodies cause so many of the changes we face in mid-life that some preventive maintenance pays dividends.

Perhaps you haven't exercised in years. Maybe you know little about nutrition. You may maintain a frantic schedule that rarely allows enough time for adequate rest. Your body reminds you of your neglect—you see the bulges and bags, and feel the fatigue and lethargy.

Here are a few simple steps to begin physical restoration and maintenance:

1. Take a walk today—or walk up and down a flight of stairs three or four times. Remember, though, it's best to start slowly.
2. Read a reliable book on nutrition such as *A Year of Beauty and Health,* by Bev and Vidal Sassoon, New York: Simon and Schuster, 1975.

3. Determine one activity you can delete from your schedule, if necessary, to allow for more rest.
4. This week do something that is emotionally relaxing or restorative for you. It could be something like:

- looking through your old photo albums
- lunch with a friend
- lunch by yourself
- taking a walk in the park or along a country lane or on the beach
- reading a book you've long put aside
- planting some flower seeds
- trying a new recipe
- window shopping
- painting a room or a picture
- taking an elderly person for a walk or a drive

What makes *you* happy? What relaxes you? What makes you feel good about yourself? Do it *this* week!

Evaluate Your Present Situation
Asking yourself the following questions and jotting down your answers will clarify your thinking.

- What troubles me now?
- What stressful event or situation demands my time?
- What captures my thinking when I go to bed at night and when I wake up in the morning?
- Who else is involved in this situation or problem?
- In what possible ways could this be resolved?
- If no resolution seems possible, what can I do to live more gracefully with the situation?

Let's consider some sample answers.

"What troubles me now? Twenty unnecessary pounds that I've carried with me about three years.

"Who else is involved? My family, because I cook and shop for them—they will have to adjust and encourage me if I'm to succeed in losing weight.

"How can this be resolved? Starting Sunday I will begin the diet my doctor gave me. Five days out of seven I will walk briskly for twenty minutes. I will ask my daughter, Kay, to accompany me on shopping trips to help me buy only the foods permitted on the diet. When eating out I will arrange with my husband to give me some signal if I exceed my diet."

Obviously, many of the complex, troubling issues of mid-life cannot be solved so easily. Problems and their solutions multiply in complexity. But thinking them through always reduces panic. If you record your thoughts you can review them later after prayer, consideration, and counsel.

Consider New Goals and Action

Goals are important in mid-life. New aims and achievements will give fresh zest to living. These goals can be in any area of life—spiritual, educational, career, marriage, civic and community, family, and personal interests.

We need to slow our pace enough to allow time to evaluate present activities and possible changes. Plan to take a few hours or a half day soon to review your responsibilities and activities. Then eliminate the unnecessary ones and add the things you feel are important. If you can, do this away from home so your time will be uninterrupted. Go to a local library, or ask the church secretary if you can use a room at church.

You may find it helpful to use a chart like Figure 2-1 on page 48.

ACTIVITY EVALUATION CHART

Activity	Essential	Desirable	Questionable	Unnecessary

Figure 2-1

When you've completed your evaluation discuss it with your husband and family if any decisions involve them.

Finding unnecessary activities and saying no can be difficult. But once we have determined the important things in our lives and have prayed over them, we must take the initiative to eliminate other things which don't meet the goals and priorities we have set.

Evaluate *at least* once a year, but preferably once every six months or every three months. New activities and responsibilities accumulate rapidly if we don't keep a tight rein on our schedules. Never let the good things of life crowd out the best.

Mid-life can present women with some of their most productive and rewarding years of life—living to the fullest, experiencing the joy of God's presence, and having stable, happy relationships with others.

Mid-life can mean closing the door on unproductive activities and past mistakes and viewing new vistas eagerly and hopefully. God does give new opportunities and fresh starts.

NOTES: 1. James Dobson, *Hide or Seek* (Old Tappan, New Jersey: Fleming H. Revell Co., 1974), page 15.
2. Robert D. Foster, *Seven Minutes with God* (Colorado Springs, Colorado: NavPress, n.d.).

CHAPTER 3

Men in Mid-life

It had been a good day. The entire family was asleep and the house was cooling with the February night. Mary was asleep beside me. Snug between the sheets and blankets I was warmly comfortable. It was a good time to think, and I did—about many things. I began reviewing where I was in life. I thought about aging, mid-life, and my next birthday. *Three score and ten years. Well, I have half of my life yet to live.* Then I came alert with a start. *That's not true. I'm almost forty-two—seven years over the halfway mark. Eight more years to my half-century!*

In that moment I realized I had mentally suspended myself at age thirty-five. It was only then I realized I was clinging to youth and not fully recognizing I had reached mid-life.

But I should have noticed it earlier. That inevitable roll of fat fights with my belt for position. Gray hairs balance the brown in number. I find myself less daring physically, and muscular aches are more pronounced. Being around our teenage children and their friends vividly emphasizes my lack of youth.

Yet youth is so hard to give up—even though we have

no choice. We live in a youth-oriented culture. A friend in the personnel business recently told me that by the time a man is twenty-six to twenty-nine you can tell if he will make it as an executive. That could be discouraging to one who is long past that age.

Reflecting on age, Henry Still comments,

> There comes a day—perhaps a chill, damp dawn in autumn—when it is more difficult to spring out of bed and face the work of the world. You feel a twinge of stiffness in knee or shoulder. Dry skin flakes when you scratch. Sitting on the edge of the bed, reluctant to meet the day, you contemplate blue veins on ankle or calf and brown pigment spots on the back of your hand.
>
> There has been a change in the weather, you note absently, signaled by soreness in the pink slash of scar where the gallbladder came out last year. Dawn provides a moment to wonder how high your blood pressure is today and the cholesterol. You can't quite remember what it was you told yourself last night not to forget this morning.
>
> A bathroom mirror is cruel at dawn. It reveals a roll of fat around the body, loose skin under the chin, and gray in the stubble before the lather goes on.[1]

The realization that our youth is slipping away startles many of us to varied emotional reactions. Some are fearful. Others push and work harder. Some try to dress and act young. Some exercise frantically. Many give up. But all inevitably lose the battle and crash into mid-life—perhaps kicking and screaming against its pull.

A man's mid-life motivation and the problems he faces differ signficantly from what a woman must deal with. Career tasks predominate in his mid-life experiences because he cannot stop functioning as a breadwinner for the family. He thinks he is trapped. He has a sense of being imprisoned, and escape is impossible.

As a man experiences his mid-life transition he suddenly faces unfamiliar issues. He begins to ask if he chose the right career. He reviews his past and compares it with the dreams and goals he once pursued. He looks at his marriage and wonders why it doesn't meet his expectations. He avoids the mirror which reveals obvious physical changes. He begins to doubt his abilities and potential. In short, he begins a total reappraisal of his life.

But this questioning need not be bad. In fact, failure to go through it may well rob a man of a significant opportunity.

It certainly is not mandatory to have some traumatic crisis in mid-life. In fact, some may not sense any difficulty at all. But even when there is no crisis, changes still take place in a man's life and he must respond and adjust to them. He could decline rather than develop, but it need not be so. He is in the midst of a major reappraisal of his life and, with a proper perspective, he will emerge a new man.

Yet the turmoil of the time confuses him. As Daniel Levinson aptly observes,

> For the great majority of men . . . this period
> evokes tumultuous struggles within the self and with
> the external world. Their Mid-Life Transition is a time
> of moderate or severe crisis. Every aspect of their lives
> comes into question, and they are horrified by much
> that is revealed. They are full of recriminations against
> themselves and others. They cannot go on as before,
> but need time to choose a new path or modify the old
> one.

Because a man in this crisis is often somewhat irrational, others may regard him as 'upset' or 'sick'. In
most cases, he is not. The man himself and those who
care about him should recognize that he is in a normal
developmental period and is working on normal mid-
life tasks. The desire to question and modify his life
stems from the most healthy part of the self. The
doubting and searching are appropriate to this period;
the real question is how to best make use of them.[2]

There is hope. There are solutions for the countless
problems that spring up in mid-life. These problems had
their roots in a man's earlier years, but develop fully in the
fertile ground of physical and emotional changes in mid-
life.

And just as his decisions in late adolescence and early
adulthood influenced his life for the coming decades, so
now what he does in mid-life will determine his lifestyle for
the next twenty or thirty years. His decisions now will
greatly affect his career, his marriage, and his eventual
fulfillment in retirement. He must not pass up the opportunity to grow, or ignore the reality of the pain felt in the
process in growing.

Most authorities agree that the major life areas for a
man are his career and family—in that order. Others are
important, but these two dominate as driving forces. I
would add a third area that most secular sources ignore—
the spiritual dimension. It is key, for it gives perspective
and power. His spiritual life reshapes and refines the basic
fabric of a man's existence. Treating career, family, and
other areas without a spiritual focus touches only symptoms—relieving the outward pain, but failing to deal with
root causes. Mid-life crises must be examined in the context of spiritual development.

Career

I once had a discussion with an Air Force colonel during his last assignment before he retired at about age forty-five. I asked what he planned to do. His reply startled me: "My problem is that I haven't really decided what to do when I grow up." I laughed, but his statement was a perceptive one for a man of his age.

Growth is the key. In his career it is imperative for a man not to sense he has been embalmed and buried in his job. He must see growth—in pay, variety of work, benefits, position, and recognition. But even with growth, he may still feel unfruitful and unmotivated in his career.

A man's identity is welded to his job. After the question, "What is your name?" another follows almost invariably, "What do you do?" We categorize and pigeonhole people by their work, especially men. A carpenter, a lawyer, a doctor, a draftsman, an engineer, a factory worker—all conjure up a mental picture of the person. From this picture a man builds his self-image and tends to become what he and others expect him to be.

We all agree that this process is wrong. The personality and worth of a man is not derived from his job, but from his character. Certainly this is true in God's sight.

Consider the typical history of a man's work. In his teens he alternately dreams about and dreads working on his own. In his late teens and early twenties he prepares by experience and education. Often he takes a shot in the dark, for how can he know what he really wants to do? So he propels himself out into a career.

In his twenties he becomes totally independent of his family, begins developing in his job, and may start a family of his own. It is a hectic time of change and preoccupation with finding his place in the world. He may return to school, change jobs, or even fail at something. Yet he experiences little emotional turmoil because the resiliency of youth carries him through.

He generally enters his life's work by his late twenties or early thirties and aggressively pursues promotion, pay raises, or other kinds of security, reward, and stability in life. To this point his career still dominates his thinking, with some emphasis on his family and marriage.

Then by thirty-five or forty, several things begin to happen. A man now knows himself well enough to perceive (though perhaps not admit to himself) that his job future is limited in terms of promotion, success, and creativity. He is no longer a "promising young man." He is now expected to pull his own weight and produce. He may be bound by limitations in his ability or education. Yet he is keenly aware of his need to concentrate on "making it," as Levinson says, by achieving something in the way of position, comfort, or security.

If his struggle to this point has been financial, the pursuit of security will be most important. If finances have been adequate, comfort and position dominate. In his mind there is some kind of ladder which he must climb. Levinson describes this ladder as "all dimensions of advancement—increases in social rank, income, power, fame, creativity, quality of family life, social contribution —as these are important for the man and his world." The result is a striving "to become a senior member in one's world, to speak more strongly with one's own voice, and to have a greater measure of authority."[3]

In many jobs the remaining rungs on the ladder disappear. There is no place left to climb. In other jobs the ladder is there, but a man lacks the ability or drive to climb it. Or his job may be boring or unfulfilling, or marred by conflicts and bad relationships. In either case a sense of failure and despair emerges. The stark realization of his limitation initiates a crisis.

Other work-related factors which may signal a mid-life crisis include a wounded pride, a sense of failure, and financial insecurity.

Wounded Pride

"Pride goes before destruction, a haughty spirit before a fall" (Proverbs 16:18). Wounded pride can easily drive a man to some form of depression. When he finds he has limitations or that his potential is at an end, his ego will be hurt. But he does not like to admit his pride or be confronted with it in his job. He may tend to overrate his youthfulness and build and unfounded level of pride. But reality will later shatter his assessment.

Failure

No one is totally successful in everything he does. Failure is common to every man. Not making the basketball team in high school may be a severe blow to an athletically-minded teenager, but it appears minor in retrospect. Not being accepted by a particular university can also be a painful failure to some degree. But in the key areas of family and career, failure is particularly distressing for a man, especially in mid-life.

Yet failure is one of the chisels which God uses to shape a man into his image for greater use later. Many men go through their early adult life scrambling for success at any price instead of balancing career goals with family and personal needs. Consequently, they pay a high price for success. An initial sense of fulfillment soon gives way to emptiness when they realize they have failed with their family or in the personal dimension of their lives.

For most men, mid-life will coincide with a sense of

failure at work—perhaps as minor as a delayed promotion, a gentle reprimand, or a missed opportunity; or as great as being fired, rebuked, or obviously surpassed by younger men. Demands for excessive overtime or being given tasks beyond their ability can also contribute to a sense of failure. But whatever the failure it must be evaluated in the context of the total mid-life experience.

In 2 Timothy 4, Paul could well have sensed failure in his mission as he wrote from prison:

> At my first defense, no one came to my support, but everyone deserted me. . . .But the Lord stood at my side and gave me strength, so that through me the message might be fully proclaimed and all the Gentiles might hear it. And I was delivered from the lion's mouth (2 Timothy 4:16-17).

Paul clearly saw that God's purposes were being accomplished even in discouraging circumstances.

Failure may be the very thing that causes a man to reassess his entire life structure and future. It also drives us to God and fosters a new dependence on him, as expressed in Psalm 119:67 and 71. "Before I was afflicted I went astray, but now I obey your word. . . . It was good for me to be afflicted, so that I might learn your decrees."

Financial Uncertainty

In mid-life financial pressures intensify. Teenagers' clothing, college tuition, music lessons, a larger house, the desire for more security or comfort, and a host of other demands drain our financial resources just at a time when income may be leveling off.

During his early years a man sacrificed, tightened his belt, and rationalized financial security as a step to something better. But in mid-life he responds more intensely. A crisis can be ignited by an unexpected medical bill, overextending to buy a home, a move, the loss of a job, or a threat to security.

Financially obligations can force a man to stay on a job he detests and keep him from starting out on a new life direction. They can make him compromise his standards of ethics to keep his job. They can precipitate family arguments and turmoil. The pressure to maintain or increase his level of income can make a man feel trapped in a career at a time when he most desires a change. Even the man who draws a large salary generally spends it all or takes risks in investments which produce the pressure of uncertainty and anxiety.

Other factors in work may signal a mid-life crisis for a man. Issues like interpersonal conflict, pressure to produce, demands to move or quit, pressure to work excessive overtime, tasks beyond his ability or career, dissatisfaction and boredom all may strike an open nerve and produce a crisis situation. And, for a man, it will be a pivotal point of his life. The book *Your Job: Survival or Satisfaction?* offers significant help in specific situations of work.

The first step in coping with a career-related mid-life crisis is to avoid impulsive moves Instead, give careful thought to rebuilding yoiur life's structure and goals. Concentrate on basic values and issues, not on feelings and incidents. Give the highest priority to reviving your spiritual foundations.

Marriage and the Family

As his career dreams begin to warp and crack, a man opens his eyes to a new perspective on his wife and children.

Often he awakens too late, after his family has lived many years in the shadow of his work and personal ambitions. Now a new loneliness sets in as he sees his needs and inadequacies as a husband and father. It may take a jolt in his career to reveal this deeper and more significant need.

Several years ago I took my family on a camping vacation in California. Just before we left home my company underwent a sudden change in management with the subsequent likelihood of reorganization. Most probably I would be asked to move to a new location. The vacation was a noticeable progression from one phone booth to another as I kept abreast of developments. I was unable to sleep at night—a rare thing for me. Thoughts, ideas, and deep emotions kept me unsettled but not about my job or our possible move. I was disturbed about how little time I had left with my high school son, Steve, and how many things I had failed to do for him and with him. I was troubled.

After a couple of nights of turmoil I sat down in a forest campground in California and wrote out my thoughts. I made some plans and commitments. Then I was totally at peace and we continued our vacation. In my case, a possible change of job circumstances highlighted a need in my family and caused me to reevaluate my priorities and lifestyle.

Most men choose wives who can share their dreams of the future. Their marriage begins on an idealistic note, but reality sets in as the struggle of marital adjustment ensues. If the marriage survives the early tests, stability usually prevails to mid-life. Then another reassessment process begins which can lead to severe conflict and crisis. Some aspects of this reassessment impinge especially on the man.

Lust

Though sexual lust is present much earlier, it appears

with special force in mid-life. As a man sees his wife growing older she can become less desirable in his eyes, particularly if they have had poor communication and an unsatisfying sexual relationship. He begins looking around
and being tempted by other women who meet the picture
of his fantasies. As uncertain feelings and a changing self-
image develop in mid-life he is more vulnerable to sexual
promiscuity and marital infidelity. Many men try to escape
through pornography or X-rated films, which simply
heighten their dissatisfaction.

It is imperative to be aware of the invasion of lust in
mid-life and put up a special guard against it.

Divorce

An increasing number of divorces are occurring in the
mid-life period. In the struggle to discover new goals and a
new life many men opt to abandon their marriage. Reasoning, logic, and even love cannot persuade them to stick it
out and work through any difficulties.

In the United States half of all marriages end in
divorce. Christian marriages have been largely spared in
the past, but this is rapidly changing. More and more
Christians are bailing out of their marriages. They admit it
is wrong, but refuse to keep their commitment to seeing
their problems through. The tragic result is that children
are irreparably hurt as the innocent bystanders caught in
the backlash of adult irresponsibility.

As the spiritual head of the family, the husband is
primarily responsible for taking the lead in reconciliation
rather than taking the easy route of divorce.

Teenagers

Just at a time when many difficult issues converge on
a man, his children become teenagers and introduce a com-

pletely new set of demands and conflicts. This can have the effect of awakening a man to a new set of responsibilities. He will either help his teens become adults or he will withdraw, leaving the work of raising the family to his wife. In either case he experiences a unique set of stresses.

Children may seem to be a hindrance to a man's career and self-development. But they can be the catalyst for his greater happiness and growth.

Death of a Parent

The death of a parent frequently occurs in mid-life. This can be extremely difficult for a man (or a woman), especially if the relationship with the parent has been poor. It will also cause him to reflect on the reality of his own mortality. His sense of loss may be far beyond what he expected, and this can trigger a reappraisal of his direction in life. The deaths of other close relatives (a brother or sister especially) can have a similar effect.

Physical Changes

He ruffles through the Yellow Pages intent on finding something, not knowing quite where to look. "Gymnasiums, Sports, Weight—ah, there it is: Health Clubs." He joins one. He chooses clothes that make him look thinner and sportier. He dons body jewelry and loosens the top two buttons of his shirt. He tries to be tanned earlier and longer. Like many of us, he clings to a more youthful image as he gets older.

The most obvious signals of middle age are changes. Try as we may to avoid them, they come and reveal to all that we are no longer young.

What attitude should characterize the Christian man

as he grows older? Should he "let himself go?" Should he ignore his age and keep living the life of a young man? Should he adopt vain habits and artifices to cover up? Let's look at the major physical issues and then consider a few suggestions for coping with the changing physical body.

Appearance

Most men over thirty-five find themselves almost constantly engaged in "the battle of the bulge." In our well-fed society, men who do not face this battle are rare. Even those who never previously faced the problem of being overweight, will see fat appear on each side of their waist. Excess weight can be controlled by exercise and diet. But it is disconcerting to even the most secure man to see it develop. Ignored, it can lead to a severe weight problem and possibly other health concerns.

I have often caught myself staring remorsefully in the mirror at my waist. My eyes—and my pride, unfortunately —focus on the extra appendage there. Although I hate it, I'm not sure I hate it enough to permanently cut back those eight pounds I know I do not need. Yet a mixture of pride and my need for discipline remind me that I am getting older and that habits I develop now will control much of my later life.

But a change in a man's waistline is simply one of many physical changes taking place. Gray starts to invade his hair or his hair begins to fall out—or both. His face begins to lose its youthful smoothness and texture. His muscles become soft. His youth cannot be retrieved.

Energy and Endurance

A man's decreasing energy and strength can be even more distressing than changes in his appearance. In mid-life a man's body is simply not as resilient as it once was. The attempt to "burn the candle at both ends" results in continuous fatigue and illness, whereas before a good night's rest seemed to repair the entire body system.

This decrease in energy and strength especially affects those whose work includes much physical labor. Carpenters, plumbers, dockworkers, farmers, and many others may care little about their physical appearance, but are greatly affected by decreasing strength because their livelihood depends on it. Sadly, many employers care little about a man's age and physical condition. Often they demand the same amount of work and output from the fifty-year-old as the twenty-five-year-old.

At mid-life a man must take extra care to remain healthy and in good physical condition or his energy reserves will drop drastically low. Many men find themselves too tired after a day's work to be involved in anything else. Their spiritual outreach, family life, and the sexual relationship in marriage all suffer.

Even though energy and physical strength decrease as we grow older, another resource often increases—endurance. The youth spends his energy in vigorous rushes of activity and soon wears out. But endurance is staying power—the ability to keep going under adverse conditions. It involves physical strength and energy, but also, more importantly, mental and emotional stamina. And these come from experience.

In mid-life we must direct our energies. It is possible to be far more effective than we ever were in our youth, when our energy was often spent inefficiently. It is the wise use of one's energy that counts.

A Plan for Physical Development
Why should a man concern himself with his health

and his personal appearance? Some wrong motives are wanting to remain young-looking, a fear of aging, or the desire to be sexually attractive.

But the Scriptures describe our bodies as temples of the Holy Spirit, and God gives us the strength to discipline ourselves physically in order to glorify him in our bodies.

An attractive appearance will not detract from our testimony for Christ. And our appearance has much to do with a proper self-image—that is, how we reflect the image of God. Our outward appearance often suggests what we are inside. When we are down, we tend to be sloppy and careless unless good habits intervene. When we are on top spiritually we may take more care with our dress and personal appearance.

To glorify God we do not have to be super athletes, but simply fit and healthy. Our motive should be to serve God effectively. This was partly what Paul meant in 1 Corinthians 9:27—"I beat my body and make it my slave." Paul also reminded us that God has given us a spirit of self-discipline (2 Timothy 1:7), and this applies both physically and spiritually.

Thus, our good appearance and health are grounded not in personal glory, but in God's glory. With this in mind, here are some specific suggestions for physical development in mid-life:

1. Dress neatly and well, avoiding fads and outlandish clothing. Dress appropriately for your age.
2. Pay close attention to personal hygiene—shaving, body odor, teeth, nails, and clean clothing. No one may notice your cleanliness, but they certainly will notice the lack of it.
3. Eat properly. Begin cutting down on quantity since you need less. Avoid junk food and pay attention to

your nutritional needs.
4. Develop a program of regular physical exercise which meets your personal needs. Try to attain a resting pulse rate of under seventy beats per minute. Do enough muscular exercise to maintain muscle tone and to protect yourself from back strains and pulled muscles.
5. Begin having a physical examination yearly.
6. Learn to pace yourself emotionally and physically, by getting proper rest and nutrition. Avoid extremes. You don't need to run a marathon, be twenty pounds under the average weight for your age and height, or go to bed every night at nine. Simply use good sense and exercise discipline to keep yourself fit.

Spiritual Patterns in Mid-life

For a Christian man, mid-life can pose many spiritual problems as he questions the "why" of his circumstances. It can bring severe spiritual decline or significant growth. Let us outline various patterns of what can happen before, during, and after a mid-life crisis.

Strong Faith—Falling Away—Renewal

Some Christians accept Christ early in life and are active and outgoing in their faith. Then in a mid-life crisis their faith is shaken and they become bitter and questioning, falling away from their walk with God. This may continue for several months or years, resulting in a break with their church and other Christians. This falling away may result in divorce, poor relationships with children, and the lack of a personal spiritual ministry. Yet many men persist in their spiritual rebellion until some major incident is used by God to get their attention. As they see the futility of their actions, the truth of Scripture reclaims them and they return to a renewed walk with God. Their later years bring a new strengthening of their life and ministry.

Non-Christian—New Faith—New Life

Some men who go through young adulthood as a non-Christian discover in a mid-life crisis that God has real answers for the problems of life. They receive Christ as Savior and this begins a new life for them. They go through mid-life with a new foundation, and on to mature adulthood as a fruitful Christian.

Strong Faith—Falling Away—Spiritually Dead

The most disastrous possibility is the strong Christian who encounters a mid-life crisis, becomes bitter and rebellious, and turns away from God permanently. He knows God's power and still turns away. Very likely, some subtle or hidden sin had surfaced to undermine his relationship with God. He refuses to repent and return to God and sin increases its hold on his life. His early years of faith have been overturned and replaced by later years of foolish disobedience.

Nominal Faith—Falling Away—Renewal

Some men accept Christ as their Savior early in life but have not developed their relationship with him. They have never known the reality of deep commitment. They are easily disturbed by mid-life crises because their faith has never been grounded in the Scriptures and in personal experience with God. Then in a crisis they turn to God in desperation and for the first time begin to understand that God can meet any need in life. They commit their lives to Christ and acknowledge him as Lord and this leads to a life of spiritual fruitfulness.

Strong Faith—Trial—Increased Fruitfulness

The ideal pattern is for a man to grow deeply in his youth and as a young adult, experiencing fulfillment in his walk with Christ. Then in mid-life, as transitions come, he sinks his roots even more deeply into the Scriptures. He uses the mid-life experience as a time of growing in dependence on God. He emerges as a more mature man whose greatest fruitfulness is still in the future.

Life Goals and Self-esteem

Only a few people write out their short-term or life goals, yet everyone has them. Each man somehow sets his mind and heart on a certain target toward which he aims. It may not seem well-defined to other people or to himself. But from his youth he dreams and wishes for something unique in his life—some accomplishment that satisfies him deeply. He may be unable to express it even to his wife. But his yearning for some future fulfillment usually grows steadily.

A man may not be overly idealistic or ambitious in his goals. It could be a good job, a problem-free family, successful children, financial security, or a house of his own. For others it may be promotion, wealth, position, owning a company, or political power.

The size of the goal or its significance to other goals matters less than a man's perception of where he is in relation to achieving it. But few men reach their goals, and during mid-life they realize they will fall short. Confusion and doubt set in—even for the Christian: *Was it the wrong goal? Where did I fail? Should I keep trying? Can I carve out a new direction?* Even when a man reaches his goal, he may sense a lack of fulfillment and feel compelled to set fresh goals which may prove unattainable.

Related to the achievement of goals is a man's overall self-esteem. His view of himself may become more realistic in mid-life and he may begin looking down on himself and losing confidence for the future. This is often a result of having improper goals—or at least improper motives behind good goals.

Improper Goals

Many men spend their energies and lives pursuing and achieving a goal only to find that it has no lasting meaning. They are left empty and dissatisfied. In fact, they may find their goal directly opposed to the things in life that matter most.

Certain goals are particularly destructive:

1. *Materialism.* With a materialistic goal no amount of success will actually satisfy. Money, furniture, homes, cars, and clothes may seem immediately important, but they have no lasting value. The world measures a man's success largely by his accumulation of money and possessions. One need not possess much to lust for "more." A materialistic drive infects rich and poor alike.

   Scripture teaches that spiritual goals should occupy our lives. "Do not store up for yourselves treasures on earth, where moth and rust destroy, and where thieves break in and steal. But store up for yourselves treasures in heaven, where moth and rust do not destroy, and where thieves do not break in and steal. For where your treasure is, there your heart will be also" (Matthew 6:19-21). All financial goals should be in the context of spiritual goals.

   Unfortunately, many men spend several years of their working lives primarily pursuing materialistic goals. Then they discover this fallacy and experience disappointment. As one very successful man put it, "There I was, on the threshold of nothing!"

2. *Selfishness*. In Mary's and my experience we have observed that men are far more self-centered than women. Most women spend their early years *giving* to others, especially their family in terms of time and energy. Men spend their early years *getting*—a job, money, a promotion, and things. Often their selfishness is closely related to materialism. Yet it is more than just the materialistic orientation that is wrong. When any goal is only self-centered it will ultimately become self-destructive. No man can live only for himself without eventually becoming an empty, bitter person. Looking out for number one is a poor motto and in opposition to God's commands. Rather, "Do nothing out of selfish ambition or vain conceit, but in humility consider others better than yourselves. Each of you should look not only to your own interests, but also to the interests of others" (Philippians 2:3-4).

3. *Lack of Spiritual Focus*. All goals, no matter how noble and unselfish, lose their meaning when a man has no spiritual focus in life. Focus is a good word to describe this concept for it denotes sharpness of image and a specific direction. Many Christian men desire general spiritual involvement, but their goals in this area vary from being fuzzy to nonexistent.

It is not sufficient to include God as an afterthought in our lives. He demands the center place. Many of our goals are wrong because we have not put Christ first in a specific way. "But seek first his kingdom and his righteousness, and all these things will be given to you as well." (Matthew 6:33).

Building a New Life Structure

When a man's goals and ambitions crumble, the way he has structured his life begins to collapse as well. It is frightening for him to realize this is happening. His self-esteem plunges. He often loses self-confidence and doubts his abilities. He may change jobs or careers, undergo a personality change, have an affair, and get divorced. He breaks out of his old life to seek new goals which may be just as vain as his old ones.

Building a new and lasting life structure does, of course, require a rethinking of goals and values. It forces a man to realistically ask, "What is really important to me at this time in my life? Where do my children and family fit? How important is my career? What have I missed in my past? Where do spiritual goals fit?" These questions form the core for a rebuilding process. As a man answers them, he will see new directions for a fulfilled life.

Signals of a Mid-life Crisis

Some kind of major change will take place in most people's lives during mid-life. For those who approach it in a spiritual and positive manner, the elements of a crisis may not exist. For others this major change unfolds with a series of disturbing events.

We fear what we do not know or understand. That is why illness often frightens us since we do not really understand what is happening in our body. When a man understands some of the signals of a mid-life crisis he can face it and deal with it constructively. The following list of crisis indicators is by no means universal. Some men experience only one, while others may experience many of them all at once or over a period of a few years.

Panic about Success

In our surveys, the majority of mid-life crises in men were directly related to their careers. One of the first indicators for a man that a mid-life transition is impending is a panicky desire to succeed. This may be evidenced by a sense of approaching failure, a realization that he has "peaked out", a feeling that time is running out to "make it" in the job, being passed over for some promotion, or feeling an extraordinary pressure to produce. The result of his feelings is an urge to work harder and a fear that his job or career is jeopardized.

External evidences of a mid-life crisis are longer working hours, giving the job priority over everything else, neglecting the family and spiritual matters because of "having" to work, and nervousness or irritability with co-workers. The root of this panic is the underlying fear of failure.

Lack of Motivation

Another indicator of a possible mid-life crisis is a growing lack of motivation in a man's career. This is the opposite reaction to being panicked to succeed. This lack of drive appears mainly on the job, but spills over into other areas of life such as family involvements and spiritual and physical fitness.

A man experiencing this must ask himself, "What motivates me?" His motivation may be wrongly derived from promotion, money, power, or success; and because these are ultimately without significant value, they will eventually disappoint him. But the worthwhile motivation which stems from the desire to support one's family, contributing to a worthy cause, or to influence other men towards a relationship with Jesus Christ, will continue even when job circumstances change.

Depression

Depression is certainly not unique to mid-life. In our surveys, it was the way most men and women responded to a crisis in their middle years. Depression is especially difficult when a person has not experienced it before.

Sexual Lust

Most men associate sexual prowess with youthfulness, and they fear losing their sexual ability as their youth fades. Combined with decreasing job satisfaction, a so-so marriage, and a new need to prove himself, the temptation to infidelity can easily overcome a man in mid-life. With a sense of abandon and desperation some men (Christians and non-Christians alike) form illicit relationships with women which build their wounded egos.

Frequently this process begins when a woman friend listens as he describes the inner struggles he is encountering. Unfortunately, a few moments of such indiscretion can lead to tragic changes in marriage, reputation, and spiritual influence. Many godly, spiritually mature men have fallen to this temptation only to find that its sweetness and satisfaction turned into bitterness, depression, and a ruined life and marriage.

Emotional Changes

A significant change in your emotional expression can indicate an approaching mid-life crisis. A man who rarely lost his temper in the past may find himself suddenly prone to anger and irritability. Similarly, one who is usually outgoing and people-oriented may find himself becoming moody and withdrawn.

Fear

An onslaught of fears can be another signal. A man

may fear financial or other failure, losing a job, or his children becoming rebellious. Similarly, an unusual focus on security can make a man bury himself in a job that smothers him. Should he lose it, he knows that his age may prevent him from quickly being hired elsewhere. He also becomes more conscious of retirement, and life insurance. This is certainly not wrong, but it is a clear signal that a new era of life is approaching.

Practical Suggestions

Understand Yourself

In mid-life you will have the opportunity to learn more about yourself than ever before. You have lived long enough to develop a realistic estimate of your abilities and gifts. You have had enough failure to know you are vulnerable, but still have enough optimism to set new directions.

The key to taking advantage of this time is to look objectively at your past and the present and to understand where you are in life now. Also try to understand the additional changes that may come soon, and be prepared for them.

This is an excellent time to take aptitude or temperament tests like the Taylor-Johnson Temperament Analysis Test (many pastors are trained to give them). Do everything you can to develop a grasp of your personality, abilities, and strengths. Your wife can be your best source of objective evaluation as well as personal encouragement.

Renew Your Spiritual Commitments

This is a prime time to make or renew your commitments to God. Set spiritual goals for yourself and your family. Above all, spend time daily reading the Scriptures and praying. You need God's help in realigning your life, but prayers can be empty and pointless if they deal only with an immediate problem rather than a deeper relationship with God. Mid-life can be either the richest spiritual time of your life or the time when you shut God out and pursue your own direction. It must be a conscious choice. There is no middle ground.

Redirect Your Goals

Use this time to rethink your goals in light of biblical principles and your personal needs. Analyze what kind of goals you had before and make any necessary changes. Ask these questions:

- What was right about my previous goals?
- What was wrong with my previous goals?
- What are my needs now?
- What new goals do I need?

Take Time

Change does not happen overnight. At this turning point of your life an impulsive decision could be disastrous. Take time to think and pray. Write down your thoughts. Take extra time with your wife and children to help you focus on what is meaningful. Try to schedule short vacations to get away with your wife to relax, pray, think, and talk. And remember that the emotions, problems, and crises of the moment can change with time. Be patient, and allow God to develop your character and redirect your thinking and future. Of course, you cannot drop out of life and simply disappear for a year—nor would you want to. God will use the pressures of life to mature and deepen you.

Realign Your Priorities

After setting new goals, you need to make your priorities in life fit them. Not only must you *know* what is most important in your life, but you must *do* what is most important. Your goals may cause you to spend more time with your wife or children, to set aside a daily time with God, to take a more active role in your church, to reduce time spent watching television, or to reduce your work time. The key is to do what is most important first.

Find and Be a Mentor

A mentor is a person who guides, teaches, advises, and sponsors another. Usually it is an older man who takes us under his wing and shows us the ropes. He is old enough to not be a competitor, but near enough in age to be able to empathize and communicate with us. I can name four or five men who have had this kind of influence in my life.

As we grow older we tend to leave our mentors. But in mid-life we may have a great need for a mentor in the spiritual realm—one who counsels and teaches us to apply biblical truth to our daily lives.

Another of the most satisfying aspects of mid-life is to be a mentor for someone else—at work and in the church. The tendency of mid-life is to turn inward, but the best therapy is to turn outward and give yourself to others.

Develop Deeper Friendships

In a mid-life transition, friendship can provide great emotional encouragement. Most friendships are formed in our younger years. As a man grows into mid-life he often becomes more independent, more superficial in his relationships, and more reserved in sharing his inner thoughts. His friends from earlier years could furnish great support in his mid-life, but it is unlikely that they are close by because of our mobile society. So at a time when there is a deep need for close male friends, he may, in fact, have almost none close enough to share his struggles and turmoil. Therefore, cultivating two or three deep friendships is important.

The ideal is for a couple to develop close friendships with other couples. Such friendships need to be based on both spiritual goals and compatible personalities. Very likely they will be formed with peers who are of similar social status and background. Take the initiative to develop the kind of friendship described in Proverbs 17:17 —"A friend loves at all times, and a brother is born for adversity."

Maintain Physical Exercise

At a time when they may need extra energy and endurance, many men in mid-life neglect physical exercise and proper diet. Yet it is not too late to start a reasonable program of diet and physical exercise to give you the physical capacity for going through the emotional conflicts of mid-life. The more out of shape you are, the less emotional and physical stamina you will have in times of stress. A few minutes of daily exercise will probably be sufficient.

NOTES: 1. Henry Still, *Man-made Men* (New York: Hawthorn Books, 1973), pages 178-179.
2. Daniel J. Levinson, *The Seasons of a Man's Life* (New York: Alfred A. Knopf, 1978), page 199.
3. Ibid., pages 59-60.
4. Jerry and Mary White, *Your Job: Survival or Satisfaction?* (Grand Rapids, Michigan: Zondervan Publishing House, 1977).

CHAPTER 4

Success and Failure

Noticing the new colonel's insignia on Tom Forster's shoulders, I congratulated him. But after a few minutes of conversation I said, "Tom, you don't seem too happy about your promotion and new assignment."

"I'm not," he replied. "I tried to resign, but the Air Force refused my resignation."

Unknown to me, Tom's life was falling apart.

Outwardly he was a success. A full colonel in the Air Force. A Ph.D. in Aeronautics. A command pilot with thousands of hours flying time. A Naval Academy graduate. Deputy Commander of a significant Air Force scientific research organization.

But inwardly he despaired. He would drive home from work at Wright-Patterson Air Force Base in Dayton, Ohio and sit in his driveway for twenty to thirty minutes trying to analyze where he had gone wrong. Work was depressing. The challenge was gone. Even his fine family was not enough.

As Tom told me later, "All that should have made me happy did no good at all. It seemed I had no friends—at least no one who really cared for me and was concerned about what I was going through."

Eventually Tom did resign from the Air Force and joined a consulting firm. A few months later his daughter Carol told her parents she had committed her life to Jesus Christ after attending a church where she heard an explanation of how to become a Christian. Tom was unmoved, but Carol told him if he ever wanted to experience Christ's living presence he should attend the church she had visited.

Four weeks later Tom's son, an outstanding gymnast, fell and broke his hip. The doctors subsequently found a tumor so large they decided his leg should be amputated just below the buttock.

"I was paralyzed," Tom told me. "My first thought was that I needed God. I remembered what Carol had said, so the following Sunday I went to her church. We were really hurting and needed help. It seemed like the sermon was just for me. It was the first time I had been in a Christ-centered church and experienced God's presence."

Tom returned to the church the next Sunday, and the pastor explained how to become a Christian. Tom prayed that Christ would enter his life and give him salvation.

Meanwhile his son was undergoing further examinations, and the doctors decided to try an operation that might save his leg. He could expect to be in a cast for several months and never compete in gymnastics again.

The operation was successful, and his son's recovery miraculous. His cast was off in seven weeks, and he was back in gymnastics a few months later—going on to win state honors in high school and earning a college athletic scholarship. Furthermore, he had become a Christian through the witness of a friend in the hospital. Tom and his son began doing daily Bible study together.

"All that struggle after achieving worldly success now

makes sense," Tom said. "I had been giving myself to the wrong things. My crisis led me to Christ."

For Tom, an overwhelming sense of failure and need led to the discovery of true success.

Not everyone responds to failure so positively. A newspaper article tells of a middle-aged man who held a responsible position with a good company. He was on his way up and seemed to have the world by the tail. He acted boldly and exuded confidence. But one day his boss called him into his office and fired him.

He subsequently obtained a good job with better pay. But one year after being fired he described it like this:

"I'd like to be able to tell you that it was a learning experience, and that I'll laugh about it some day, but I can't. I want you to know that it's the closest thing to dying I ever expect to feel. That's the only way to describe it to you. It feels like you're dying.

"I always used to just assume that everyone envied me because of the success I'd had in my work. Now, on paper, I'm just as successful—more successful monetarily—but because of that one blot, of being fired, I seem to think that I'm a failure forever and I'm afraid of people finding out. . . .

"Something inside me is saying that if I let loose and enjoy myself too much, I'm going to be yanked back to reality by being fired again. So in a lot of ways I'm not the same person. I'm working and I have a good job, but I'm not the same person. It's only been a year. Maybe it will go away. I don't know."[1]

No one likes to fail. Everyone wants to succeed. But both success and failure are fraught with danger and temptation if not handled properly. Failure can cause a person to give up and quit and to blame God for the circumstances. Success can inflate the ego and cause people to neglect God. But under God's direction, both can build us into more mature men and women.

Of course, success is a matter of perspective and attitude. Getting a $50 per month pay raise may be considered a failure because others got a $100 raise. Or it could be a success because six other employees were laid off.

We have a mania for success in our culture. We exalt the successful athlete, businessman, actor, or politician. We avoid the seeming failures. The theologian A. W. Tozer aptly wrote,

> In this world men are judged by their ability to do. They are rated according to the distance they have come up the hill of achievement. At the bottom is utter failure, at the top complete success; and between these two extremes the majority of civilized men sweat and struggle from youth to old age. . . .
>
> But in all of this there is no happiness. . . .
>
> This mania to succeed is a good thing perverted. The desire to fulfill the purpose for which we were created is of course a gift from God, but sin has twisted this impulse about and turned it into a selfish lust for first place and top honors. By this lust the whole world of mankind is driven as by a demon and there is no escape.[2]

How does God measure success? What does he want for us? He told Joshua if he meditated continually on God's law and carefully observed it, "then you will be prosperous and successful" (Joshua 1:8). Success for us as well is conditional on obedience to God's word. This is success as seen from God's perspective, not the world's.

As human beings we usually determine success in one of three ways. The first is merely the *feeling* of having succeeded. Our criteria may be vague and uncertain, yet we sense it within even though we may be entirely wrong. Our feeling may have to do with specific standards or expectations or goals we have set and now judge ourselves by, but these aims could well be unrealistic or unnecessary.

Second, we assess success or failure by *how others judge us*, or how we think they judge us. Again, this evaluation method can be wrong. Judgments by others can be as subjective and unrelated to fact as our own.

Third, *a fixed, unbiased source* can reveal our success: standardized tests, written criteria for promotion or pay raises, or requirements for an educational degree.

But ultimately, God is our only judge. His perspective on our success is all that counts. Our feelings, the opinions of others, and fixed standards can never overrule God's values.

Our Vulnerable Areas

Each of us can identify areas of life where success or failure is most important to us, although these can change as we grow older. Five areas which receive the most emphasis among men and women in mid-life are career, marriage, children, other personal relationships, and our spiritual condition.

The world most often judges success first in the realm of career. Christians often have identical standards as non-Christians in this area, and so they frequently miss success in other, equally important ways.

Failure in marriage is more emotionally upsetting than a failure in any other area of life. The commitment we make at the outset involves every facet of our life and being. A marriage relationship either grows and develops through the years or it deteriorates and leaves scars.

A middle-aged Christian man who recently divorced his wife wrote to me about the aftermath: "I guess I've had the normal ups and downs. It has been lonely at times. Also I keep re-examining things—still trying to figure out what went wrong. At this point in time I feel an acute sense of failure in probably one of the most important areas of life."

Divorce rips us apart emotionally and spiritually. Yet Christian couples have every resource and reason to succeed in marriage even though the problems become acute in mid-life.

As parents, much of our feeling of success depends on our children's successes. Our emotions go up and down as they achieve in some areas and fail in others. Elation and despair can race through our emotions all in the span of an hour as we talk with them. We are emotionally vulnerable because we have less and less control over their success and failure as they become increasingly independent and start making decisions on their own—at times in direct opposition to us.

In personal relationships outside the family, we often tend to stop growing in our ability to relate to others—at just the time when we need closer friendships.

As for the spiritual realm, there are few greater tragedies than meeting an older Christian with graying hair and a distinguished appearance and position only to find that he or she is spiritually immature. For true spiritual maturity is the key to coping with the fallout from problems in all other areas. Yet we easily neglect spiritual development. When we finally discover our need we feel it is too late to change—though it never is. No Christian should tolerate failure in the area of spiritual growth. We must succeed here.

Our success or failure in all these areas determines our self-image—the picture we have of ourselves. The picture may be inaccurate, but it is what we see and believe. Most failures and successes actually begin here—we *think* we will fail or succeed in something because of who we imagine we are. Sooner or later our thoughts emerge in reality as fulfilled prophecy.

Why Does God Allow Success or Failure?

One man is a committed Christian and a competent worker for his company. He lets God be in charge of his career. Promotion follows promotion until he advances to the company presidency. A second man is also a committed Christian and a competent worker who keeps his focus on God. But he misses promotions, and, in fact, is soon forced to leave his company. Why?

The answers for the seeming inequalities of life are not simple. They are rooted in God's grand purpose for us, something not easily understood by any of us.

But seeing this in the proper perspective first requires taking a look at the significant difference between the world's view of life and God's view of life. Consider the following:

THE WORLD'S VIEW	GOD'S VIEW
The world focuses on money, possessions, and other things which develop a person's comfort, pleasure, and pride.	God focuses on developing the inner character of a person, so that he reflects all the good qualities God himself possesses.

The world emphasizes a person's outward position, rank, or prestige.	God emphasizes the person—the infinite worth of the individual.
The world pushes for short-term gain—getting the most out of life now.	God works for a person's long-term gain—what will benefit him for his earthly life and for eternity.
The world emphasizes self-centeredness—a selfishness focused on "my" needs.	God helps us focus on the needs of others.
The world pushes for self-protection by emphasizing financial and physical security.	God teaches the need for a strong spiritual life, and that his presence with us is our true security.

The contrasts are obvious. God has a totally different goal in mind for Christians than the transient good feeling of supposed success. In the Bible we see this as a two-fold purpose: First, he wants to reconcile each person to himself through Christ's sacrifice for man's sin. Second, he wants to develop each person into Christ's image.

The former we refer to as his redemptive work on the cross, expressed in the Great Commission (Matthew 28:19-20). The latter is his developmental work in the Christian. In times of strain and in success most Christians have turned to Romans 8:28 for assurance and encouragement. "And we know that in all things God works for the good of those who love him, who have been called according to his purpose." Here we plead God's sovereignty in every circumstance. Yet this verse does not explain why we can trust his sovereignty. The answer follows in verse 29.

"For those God foreknew he also predestined to be conformed to the likeness of his Son, that he might be the
firstborn among many brothers."

A full interpretation of this verse and the surrounding
passage leads us through deep theological water. However,
at the minimum, we see that God's ultimate purpose is to
see every Christian conformed to Christ's image in their
character. Therefore, the "good" of Romans 8:28 is what
is good to God, not necessarily what we might readily view
as good. God's purpose is to develop patience, love,
humility, holiness of life, compassion, and faith in us
through every event of life.

In the Old Testament God dealt with the nation of
Israel much as he does with individuals today. Trials and
triumphs were designed by God for a specific purpose.
Deuteronomy 8:1-3 says,

> Be careful to follow every command I am giving you
> today, so that you may live and increase and may enter
> and possess the land that the Lord promised on oath
> to your forefathers. Remember how the Lord your
> God led you all the way in the desert these forty years,
> to humble you and to test you in order to know what
> was in your heart, whether or not you would keep his
> commands. He humbled you, causing you to hunger
> and then feeding you with manna, which neither you
> nor your fathers had known, to teach you that man
> does not live on bread alone but on every word that
> comes from the mouth of the Lord.

These words punctuated two great events of failure
and success. The Israelites had just experienced forty years
of wandering in the wilderness as a result of their leader's
disobedience. All the adults died in the process except

three—Moses, Joshua, and Caleb. Following that experience comes the incredibly successful invasion of the promised land. At this point God explained the reason for the failure of the last forty years and the conditions of the impending success.

Two thoughts leap off the pages of Scripture—*obedience* and *remember*. Of the two, obedience takes precedence. The Israelites wandered in the wilderness because of their disobedience. Their future success depended on a fresh commitment to obedience. Their obedience, regardless of circumstance, is the primary concern of God. This theme permeates all of Scripture. "To obey is better than sacrifice" (1 Samuel 15:22). "Whoever has my commands and obeys them, he is the one who loves me" (John 14:21). So we must obey what we know of God's word whether we are succeeding or failing. Obedience is the way out of failure. It is the way into success.

Recount how God led you in the past. The past does not ensure the future, but the past prepares us for the future. Most of us live in the existential now, somewhat like Christ's disciples in Mark 6:52. "They had not understood about the loaves [which had just occurred]; their hearts were hardened." God intends for us to recount his past blessings and lessons as preparation for the future.

We readily admit the value of obedience and remembering, but we resist the *process* of learning the lessons. In Deuteronomy 8:2 God reveals that the purpose of the failure experience was to "humble you and to test you in order to know what was in your heart, whether or not you would keep his commands." All are character development processes.

Testing assesses the strength and value of an object. Without testing we cannot really know the depth of our commitment to God. Testing produces deeper qualities of character and godliness. No testing is too great since we have the promise, "No temptation [testing] has seized you except what is common to man. And God is faithful; he will not let you be tempted beyond what you can bear. But when you are tempted, he will also provide a way out so that you can stand up under it" (1 Corinthians 10:13). Temptation and testing are closely related. In Matthew 4, Christ was tested and tempted. In most cases they are synonymous. Testing, properly responded to, develops character. Testing, improperly responded to, leads to bitterness and resentment.

"Pride goes before destruction, a haughty spirit before a fall. Better to be lowly in spirit and among the oppressed, than to share plunder with the proud" (Proverbs 16:18-19). Humility is one of life's greatest virtues and is repeatedly commended by God. Pride, its opposite, falls under God's serverest condemnation.

Thus God uses the circumstances of life, like failure, to develop humility as the focus of our character. In Micah 6:8 God says directly what he expects of every Christian. "He has showed you, O man, what is good. And what does the Lord require of you? To act justly and to love mercy and to *walk humbly* with your God."

Nothing seems to humble us quite so much as failure. And it can sometimes be the experience that turns our life in the right direction. As a young Air Force officer I entered pilot training thinking that only as a pilot could I advance. My mind was filled with the glamor of flying. Suddenly, after having done well in nine months of training, I flunked a check ride in jet formation flying. Within days I was put out of the program. I was humiliated. But it was a spiritual turning point in my life. It forced me to turn to God for my life's direction and made me stop taking things into my own hands.

In retrospect it was a minor failure. But no failure seems minor at the moment, especially in mid-life. But God's perspective remains the same. True success is built on the cornerstone of humility, and it may take failure to humble us and to develop our character.

God can also use success to develop our humility, if we view success properly. Often our success is due so little to what we have done that we are humbled to realize how God works on our behalf. But learning humility through success is far more difficult for us, since pride comes so easily when we ride a wave of success.

The final part of God's training process reveals what is really on our hearts. Again, the focus is on the inner man, the character. The external evidence of this inner character is obedience to God's word.

As Moses explained to Israel, the desired result of God's testing and humbling is that we *understand* our total dependence on God's word. Life is more than "bread"—food, possessions, position, power, even success. Life bears meaning only in obeying God's word. So again we focus on obedience.

If you are experiencing success right now, remember that God has provided it, not you. Remember also that earthly success is fleeting. Success is not our right, but only a privilege from God for a given time. This could make us fear losing it, but if our focus and dependence are on God such fear is unfounded.

A Fulfilled Life

You know the feeling: Experiencing some failure—perhaps even a minor one—you first feel shaken and almost bitter, and looking back your life suddenly seems like a series of failures. Others would quickly point out your successes, and you would too at a less depressing time. But your personal expectations were higher than your actual achievements.

One's personal measure of failure and success is determined primarily by prior expectations. Often it has little to do with reality or fact. These expectations do not remain constant throughout life. In mid-life they may differ significantly from earlier life.

What influences our self-expectations? Mostly, we would have to admit, it is others: what they expect of us or say about us, what they consider success, what we see in them that we admire and want to imitate. Such peer pressures and comparisons are wrong. However, we do have proper standards for measuring success.

At the risk of oversimplification, think of all your expectations in life as centering on the four areas shown in Figure 4-1 on page 92: your relationship with Christ, your family, your job, and your ministry.

Having a right relationship with Jesus Christ is the first and most important dimension of a truly fulfilled Christian life. "Since, then, you have been raised with Christ, set your hearts on things above, where Christ is seated at the right hand of God. Set your minds on things above, not on earthly things" (Colossians 3:1-2).

This means believing in Christ as your personal Savior. It means you are committed to a daily, in-depth walk with Christ which clearly governs the course of your life—you aren't simply going through the motions of Christian activity.

This is where many fail to lay a proper foundation. If you haven't lived a truly committed Christian life before, you won't be well prepared to handle a sudden failure in mid-life.

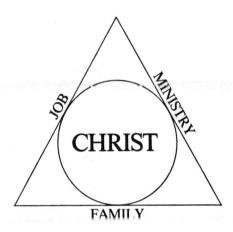

Figure 4-1

The family is the second most important dimension in a fulfilled life. "Wives, submit to your husbands . . . Husbands, love your wives . . . Children, obey your parents" (Colossians 3:18-21). Men find it easy to give their jobs higher priority than their family, while women may place more importance on the family than on their relationship with Christ. Both are wrong. No other human relationships are more important than family relationships.

The third dimension concerns our *job* and career, the fundamental purpose of which is providing for the needs of our family. When the focus becomes self-fulfillment, prestige, or wealth, we pervert the most basic purpose of work. But God does want us to enjoy what we do and he wants us to do it heartily—not for man's approval, but his. Our job is a platform for a public demonstration of the Christian life.

The final dimension is that of our ministry. We are to

reach out to others with the love and life we enjoy in Christ. "Be wise in the way you act toward outsiders; make the most of every opportunity" (Colossians 4:5). We need an outward focus as well as a relationship with Christ, our family, and our job. We should be actively involved in helping others discover life in Christ.

Avoid neglecting any of these four areas. Without Christ, our life is without a dependable, unifying force. When any of the other three areas are shortchanged, the imbalance can result in frustration and failure.

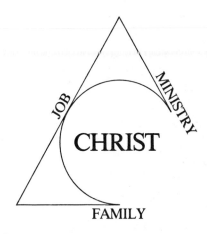

Figure 4-2

Evaluation

We need to translate subjective feelings into objective facts to evaluate true success in life. Answer the following statements to pinpoint areas of strength and areas of need.

Relationship with Christ	Yes	No
1. I have private Bible reading and prayer on at least four days a week.	___	___

2. I have done personal, written Bible study at least four times in the last six months. ___ ___

3. I have at least one friend with whom I have significant interaction on personal, spiritual issues. ___ ___

4. I have made one or more significant changes in my life in the past year in direct response to God's urging. ___ ___

5. Recent conflict with another has been resolved and is not bothering me now. ___ ___

6. So far as I know, I am not resisting God on any major issue. ___ ___

7. I have clearly received Christ as my personal Savior. ___ ___

8. I am satisfactorily established in a local church fellowship. ___ ___

Family

1. In the last month I have done some activity alone with each child. ___ ___

2. In the last month I have had some private time outside the home to spend with my spouse. ___ ___

3. In the last month I have had no more than one significant conflict with my spouse. ___ ___

4. We have had family devotions at least once in the last week. ___ ___

5. I have prayed privately with my spouse in the last month. ___ ___

6. I have not even considered divorce in the past year. ___ ___

7. I have a good relationship with my children. ___ ___

8. My job allows me enough time with my
   family.   ___ ___

Job

1. I have a job.   ___ ___
2. My basic material needs are being met.   ___ ___
3. I have been able to provide adequately
   for myself and the family.   ___ ___
4. I have never been fired.   ___ ___
5. I am basically successful in my work.   ___ ___
6. I have been promoted fairly and regu-
   larly according to merit.   ___ ___
7. I look forward to going to work most of
   the time.   ___ ___
8. I am free from any major conflicts with
   others at work.   ___ ___

Ministry

1. I now have a specific, personal ministry.   ___ ___
2. I can identify a specific spiritual gift or
   ability which God has given me.   ___ ___
3. I am using this gift or ability now.   ___ ___
4. I have between one and three major
   church responsibilities.   ___ ___
5. I have led someone outside my family to
   salvation in Christ.   ___ ___
6. I believe I am making a vital contribu-
   tion to someone's life outside my family.   ___ ___
7. I believe that God is using me now.   ___ ___

Now look back over the list. If you remember feeling a
pang of depression or fear in answering any statement, put
a check by it and plan to evaluate this area of your life
more closely. In our use of this test we have found that a

yes response to 50 percent of the statements is too low. A score between 60 and 70 percent shows a significant need.

Setting New Goals and Priorities

Failure in mid-life easily paralyzes us with a sense of fatalism making it difficult to set new goals and to get moving again. But it can be done.

The first step is to admit your need. Our natural response to failure is to cover up, pretending all is well. This deception only tears us up inside. Admit your need to God first of all, but also to a few select people. Others cannot help when they do not know of your struggles.

Recently I met an enthusiastic young couple who were living vital Christian lives in their community. The husband said that when he became a Christian he could hardly read. For years he had managed to get by. But then he realized how it was limiting him at work and in Bible study. He swallowed his pride and contacted a second grade teacher and asked her to tutor him. He met his problem head-on and took action to correct it.

To combat failure, we need to be realistic and clearly identify the area of failure. Write out the details as completely as you can to keep emotions from clouding the facts. These suggestions will also help.

1. *Guard against bitterness.* Decide not to become bitter and angry against God, yourself, or others.
2. *Recount your blessings.* Remember how God has blessed your life to this point. Thank him for the ways he can use the failure you are experiencing.
3. *Don't quit.* Determine not to let despair control you. This is more a matter of discipline than desire.

4. *Evaluate your life.* Think about where you've been and what direction you want to go in the future. Examine your family, your job, your ministry, and, most importantly, your relationship with Christ.
5. *Exercise personal discipline.* Emphasize proper rest, diet, and exercise. Increase your time in prayer and the Bible. You need these things now more than ever. God will not automatically inject you with a desire to do these things. He expects us to discipline ourselves.

Bud Ponten has had one of the most profound influences on me in the area of personal discipline. Bud is afflicted with cerebral palsy which affects both his speech and movement. For about thirty years I have observed him endure trials and experience difficulties that some would call failure. As I worked in his printing shop I saw the controlled discipline it took for him to set type. He trained himself to speak clearly by singing hymns. Competition finally forced him to close his small printing shop. Then injuries took him off another job. Year after year brought new trials. Yet his personal discipline and dependence on God prevailed. I never remember hearing him complain against God or other people despite the discouragement and depression he has experienced.

NOTES: 1. Bob Greene, "Fired Executive Lands on His Feet, But Still Feels Pain, Fear," *The Seattle Times,* August 15, 1979, page 38.
2. A. W. Tozer, *The Best of A. W. Tozer,* ed. Warren W. Wiersbe (Grand Rapids, Michigan: Baker Book House, 1979), pages 46-47.

CHAPTER 5

Depression

Martha was prominent in social activities in her city, busy in an evangelical church, well-educated, married to an understanding, loving man, but perpetually depressed.

She began sliding into occasional rounds of depression when she was thirty-two, shortly following the birth of the youngest of her three sons. Because she had always considered herself an optimistic, happy person, she was bewildered and embarrassed by the feelings of gloom and misery she experienced. She tried to talk herself out of her depression. For months she hid her distress from everyone.

Martha slept poorly. She ate little and with great effort managed to maintain her trim, appealing appearance. She went to great lengths to appear outwardly cheerful and happy while inwardly suffering the anguish of sadness and gloom.

Finally, in desperation, she talked with her doctor. "I can't understand it," she sobbed in his office. "I have everything I need to make me happy, but some days I feel so depressed that I think I can't stand it one more minute. Sometimes I've even thought of suicide. Please help me. I just can't take any more of this awful depression."

Martha's doctor gave her a thorough physical examination. He found she was slightly anemic but that did not account for her acute depression. He recommended a Christian psychiatrist.

"Oh, I couldn't go to a psychiatrist," Martha protested. "I'd be too embarrassed. What would my husband think? He would think I was crazy. I'd feel so guilty—like there was something really wrong with me."

"Martha," the doctor replied gently. "You aren't crazy, but something really is wrong and you must get help."

After a lengthy discussion Martha agreed to seek help. That evening when she hesitantly told her husband of her visit to the doctor and her appointment with the psychiatrist, a look of immense relief crossed his face. He put his arms around her.

"I knew something was troubling you," he said. "I just didn't know what to do. I'm so glad you are going to get help and I want to do whatever I can to help, too."

After a few months of weekly counseling sessions, Martha began to feel her depression lifting. The psychiatrist helped Martha discover that she constantly made high demands on herself, much higher than anyone else would expect. She felt she never measured up to her standards so she began to feel inadequate. Years of living with these thought patterns resulted in her depression.

Martha's experience is repeated millions of times yearly. The circumstances vary, the onset may be gradual or sudden, causes differ, and the intensity varies, but all depressed people suffer the same feelings.

Depression brings a real sense of suffering, often even desperation—the willingness to try anything to escape the downward spiral of unhappiness.

Because depression often invades the lives of Christians, and because mid-life presents a particular vulnerability to depression, we have devoted a chapter to it. No doubt many of our readers are experiencing depression. Christians especially fight the feelings of depression, mistakenly thinking that *all* depression is a result of sin. This adds a feeling of guilt which creates an even heavier burden by adding to the existing depression.

We do not offer a one-dimensional, simplistic approach to handling depression. For depression is almost as diverse as the people suffering from it. We will simply offer several potential causes and a few helpful suggestions which a depressed person can follow. We especially want to highlight those issues which we believe to be key in mid-life.

Scripture records many examples of godly people who struggled through seasons of depression. The story of Hannah recorded in 1 Samuel 1 shows an almost classic picture of a depressed woman. Her home situation presented constant stress. Her husband, Elkanah, had two wives. Peninnah had borne children, but Hannah had not. In the Israelite culture, a childless woman lived with disgrace. Hannah lived not only with her humiliation but also with the taunts of Peninnah. This situation existed for years. Eventually the pressure pushed Hannah into depression.

Elkanah's questions show the presence of depression's common symptoms in Hannah's life. In 1 Samuel 1:8, Elkanah asks,

- "Why are you *weeping?*"
- "Why *don't* you *eat?*"
- "Why are you *downhearted?*"

Elkanah made a few mistakes in his approach to Hannah's problem. In his love for her he tried his best to help, but he blundered by insisting that she explain her reactions. Then he went one wrong step beyond when he asked, "Don't I mean more to you than ten sons?"

Their experience illustrates what happens in a family when one person is depressed. The depressed individual desperately looks for a solution and relief, while the other family members try to change his thinking and attitudes.

In desperation Hannah poured out her sorrow and anguish to God, who alone could bring relief and a satisfactory solution.

God graciously provided Hannah with a son in response to her impassioned prayer. The prayer recorded in 1 Samuel 2:1-10 indicates that God relieved her depression. Hannah's prayer reveals strength, trust, exaltation, and rejoicing.

The depression and suffering of Job was so deep and awesome that the Scripture records in Job 2:11-13 that Job's three friends wept aloud, tore their clothes and sprinkled dust on their heads when they observed his terrible grief. Then they remained speechless for seven days and seven nights because of Job's suffering.

Paul also experienced times of sorrow and depression. In 2 Corinthians 7:5-7 he tells us of the method God used to restore his spirits.

> For when we came into Macedonia, this body of ours had no rest, but we were harassed at every turn—conflicts on the outside, fears within. But God, who comforts the downcast, comforted us by the coming of Titus, and not only by his coming but also by the comfort you had given him. He told us about your longing for me, your deep sorrow, your ardent concern for me, so that my joy was greater than ever.

God used the friendship and counseling of Titus to bring godly comfort, and relief from stress, and to restore Paul's joy.

David had bouts of depression for he records God's dealing with him during these times. "My heart is in anguish within me; the terrors of death assail me. Fear and trembling have beset me; horror has overwhelmed me" (Psalm 55:4-5). Then there is that promising statement in Psalm 23:3: "He restores my soul."

Experts continue to argue about the basic causes for depression. Many insist that the fundamental causes are biological and therefore can be treated with drugs. Others claim most depression is rooted in psychological causes and counseling therapy constitutes the effective treatment. Others attribute it to primarily spiritual problems. But to the depressed person, cause is secondary, relief is primary.

Causes of Depression

Sometimes only a single cause promotes depression, but more likely a series of causes contribute to a depressed state.

Physical Condition

Any prolonged illness may contribute to depression. Epilepsy, hyperactivity, changes in blood chemistry, thyroid malfunction, menopause, and brain changes in the elderly are some of the physiological causes.

Many people would prefer that their depression be based on a physical cause, because of their feeling of shame and embarrassment. They want to be convinced that the source of their depression is beyond their control.

Many illnesses or conditions which result in depression can be corrected with treatments which will provide relief. When seeking help for depression, always visit your physician first to check your general state of health. Often a visit to the doctor will provide a correct diagnosis. But, a word of caution here. Some doctors may be quick to prescribe drugs to mask the symptoms without attempting to deal with depression's basic causes.

Life Stresses

Psychiatrist Frederic Ilfeld has found a direct, dramatic relationship between depression and stress. Only three percent of the people who reported no social stress had high levels of depression, while 34 percent of those for whom three or more areas of their lives were stressful were very depressed.[1]

The correlation between stress and depression is great. Sometimes the stress is self-imposed and inward. Often the pressures come from without—an excessive work load, poor relationships in the home, death, divorce, or disappointments. When stress accumulates significantly, depression can result. We must all live with a certain amount of stress and pressure. In fact, pressure motivates and activates us. But when stress builds to an impossible weight, the body and mind shut down, refusing to accept any more.

A few years ago Jim celebrated his fortieth birthday. For several years preceding that birthday he had been accepting increasing responsibilities in his job and in his church. His daily routine was filled with projects and people because he was an activist by nature. Without realizing he had reached his limit, he continued to increase his pace and accept even heavier responsibilities. Then his boss suggested that he supervise one more unit in his company. To Jim's bewilderment and chagrin, he responded angrily, said "No" brusquely, left the office, and headed for home. By the time he reached his front door, his anger had diminished and was replaced with a heavy sense of despair and depression. He slumped on the couch, shoulders sagging, head down. The sensation of depression frightened him, making him feel powerless and helpless. For the first time since his mother died when he was twenty-four, he felt close to tears.

His two teenage daughters raced through the living room with two of their friends.

"Hi, Dad," one of them called. "Have a good day?"

"No," he growled as they passed.

His wife, Ellen, came down the stairs and sat beside him. "What's happening, Jim? What's wrong?"

"I don't know. I feel lousy. The boss asked me to take on more work and I said no. I can't handle any more. I feel like I'll fall apart if I have to do one more thing." He dropped his head into his hands.

"Jim, let's pray about it."

"You pray. I can't."

Ellen prayed briefly asking the Lord for wisdom and comfort. Then Jim and Ellen slowly began to talk about his situation. For a number of years Ellen had encouraged Jim to reduce his pace of living, but he had always felt he could handle more.

The next morning Jim called his pastor for an appointment and poured out his story. The pastor asked Jim to list all his current activities. Together they prayed through the list, evaluating each item and eliminating some.

Although Jim took immediate action because of his wife's urging, his depression still did not vanish. He had spent several years subjecting his body and emotions to stress, and the effects do not disappear immediately.

Months later, when his depression had subsided and his life had stabilized, Jim told Ellen, "I certainly didn't enjoy being depressed, but now I *appreciate* the depression because it gave me a new understanding of myself, a new perspective on my life, and a fresh appreciation for the comfort and healing of God."

Because of the frantic pace of life in our society, we Christians need to carefully evaluate, plan, and guard our activities, so we don't allow unimportant things to crowd our life and burden us with unnecessary stress that produces depression. It is vital to pray about our activities and ask God for his wisdom and will. "Teach me your way, O Lord; lead me in a straight path because of my oppressors" (Psalm 27:11).

Your oppressors may be an increasing burden of unnecessary stress.

Depletion of Reserves

The mid-years present us with the possibility of "living on the thin edge." There are pressures, strains, responsibilities, and demands from our family, our community, our employer, our church, even ourself, that command our attention. We give not out of an abundance of physical, emotional, and spiritual resources, but because of routine or habit. That cannot continue for long. Ultimately the facade will collapse and depression is a likely result.

In their mid-years Christians often live on spiritual experiences and blessings from their past. Spiritual stagnation and carelessness can quickly lead to guilt and depression. "Faking it" spiritually always presents problems.

God emphasized the need for sincerity and freshness in our spiritual lives when he told the people of Israel in Hosea 6:6, "For I desire mercy, not sacrifice, and acknowledgment of God rather than burnt offerings."

Empty form and ritual never satisfy. They only leave the door open for guilt and dissatisfaction.

The same is true in the emotional and physical aspects of life. We cannot continue to strain these resources unless we regularly replenish them.

If we have been strong, capable, and successful for many years we may adopt an invincible attitude. We resist the idea that we are prone to emotional collapse. We are proud and avoid admitting our limitations and inadequacies. In Galatians 6:3 Paul wrote, "If anyone thinks he is something when he is nothing, he deceives himself."

Sin and Guilt

Many Christians love God yet live in a state of depression because they have not *accepted* God's forgiveness of sin. God's word teaches us, "If we confess our sins, he is faithful and just and will forgive us our sins and purify us from all unrighteousness" (1 John 1:9).

If we are in fellowship with God and sensitive to the Holy Spirit we will know when we sin. Immediate confession should follow. The next important response is our acceptance of God's forgiveness.

Susan was forty-one and seriously depressed. When she was forty, she had quarreled bitterly with her younger brother over possessions left to them after their mother's death. They parted in anger and hostility. Later that week her brother was killed in a car accident. Susan pled with God to forgive her for her harsh treatment of her brother, but she could not accept God's forgiveness or forgive herself. The quarrel consumed her thinking and her conversations with her husband and close friends.

Finally her husband and their pastor persuaded her to see a Christian counselor. Through careful teaching he showed Susan that the *grace* of God and the *forgiveness* of

God cover every possible sin. When she understood that after sin was confessed God forgave and forgot, Susan's depression began to clear.

Unconfessed sin and oppressive guilt contribute significantly to depression. God has provided the perfect answer in confession and forgiveness.

Unresolved Hostility and Anger

In his book, *How to Win Over Depression*, Tim LaHaye says, "The first step in the chain reaction producing depression is anger. Don't be surprised that you involuntarily reject such a proposal. I have consistently observed that most depressed persons cannot and do not think of themselves as angry people."[2]

Many events occur in our life which we do not like. It's possible that by our mid-years we have accumulated anger against those who caused those events. We may also be angry with God. Often an angry, hostile person does not realize his inward reactions. He feels the right to experience such emotions because of the injustice that has been done to him.

But God never allows us the right to harbor the sin of anger and hostility. Anger is another sin we must confess to God and ask him to help us put away. If anger is not properly dealt with, the result can be depression.

Poor Self-image

Eleanor grew up in a Christian home. Her parents loved her dearly, but in their efforts to raise her to be a godly woman, they emphasized the negative traits in her life and rarely praised her for her accomplishments. They wrongly assumed too much praise would arouse her pride.

Eleanor became convinced that she was an inadequate person since she was often told so. She entered adulthood as an insecure, unhappy, self-accusing woman, ripe for depression. She covered her insecurities with a flippant, giddy exterior, but inwardly she battled with distress and self-accusation. She proved to be an excellent employee, always striving to do a better job than anyone else. She was anxious to please, dedicated, and productive. But, Eleanor felt she never did enough, that her job would always be in jeopardy unless she did more and more.

In her mid-twenties she married, and brought to the marriage all of the problems she had previously experienced. Her husband was also insecure, and a critical perfectionist, so Eleanor's life continued in much the same vein that she experienced while growing up. Eventually her flippant exterior cracked and she plunged into depression. Only after careful biblical counseling was her life turned around. She began to rebuild her life upon the basis of the word of God, gaining a new understanding of God's view of her as a worthy, acceptable individual.

Eleanor gradually learned that her self-esteem should not be based on her personal performance or on others' opinions, but on the security of God's love. She realized that her parents' and her husband's criticisms need not control her feelings. Slowly she understood she should differentiate between valid, constructive criticisms, and invalid, unnecessarily cruel criticisms. She benefited from helpful suggestions by applying them to her life. When others made cutting and cruel remarks, she recognized that the real problem lay with the overly critical individual—not her.

With a growing sense of freedom and personal well-being, Eleanor recognized, accepted, and began to enjoy God's unconditional love. She developed an attitude of thankfulness and praise.

The consistent indoctrination of a low self-esteem will

ultimately destroy an individual's emotional stability. Few of us realize how vital to our overall well-being it is to have a good view of ourself. People with a poor self-image spend more energy avoiding depression than one who has been encouraged and affirmed all his life.

Every Christian should be moving toward a better understanding and acceptance of himself regardless of his or her upbringing. By mid-life we should know the strengths and positive qualities that God has given us. While we may be annoyed or discouraged about our weaknesses, Galatians 6:4 teaches us, "Each one should test his own actions. Then he can take pride in himself, without comparing himself to somebody else." Comparisons are one of the factors which contribute most to a poor self-image.

Even if no other person ever tells us we are loved, we are special, we are worthy, we can be certain that we are because God says so. God emphasized this to the people of Israel in Jeremiah 31:3 when he said, "I have loved you with an everlasting love; I have drawn you with loving-kindness." And again in John 10:14, "I am the good Shepherd; I know my sheep and my sheep know me."

Isn't it encouraging to realize that God knows us and loves us? He knows our limitations, but also sees our potential.

It is difficult to overcome a poor self-image, especially if it is constantly reinforced by the nagging of a thoughtless mate, friend, or parents. However, we do need to accept valid criticism with grace and appreciation and take steps to change. If we honestly find the criticism unwarranted, we can ignore it.

Let's never fall into the self-defeating trap of blaming another person—our parents, our mate, our employer—for a poor self-image. God holds us alone responsible for our attitudes. Others may have bombarded us with criticism, aggression, hostility, and censure, but God restores and repairs broken lives and emotions. Sometimes several of the previously mentioned causes combine to bring depression in force. Perhaps an illness starts the depression, then the loss of a close friend aggravates it. It is difficult to personally determine the source. When a counselor or trusted friend steps in, the depressed person has help in finding the source and taking steps towards recovery.

Because depression results from many complex factors the cause may even elude counselors. Then the depressed person needs to press ahead with a recovery plan anyway, trusting God for a healing work.

Symptoms of Depression

We don't have to be taught what depression is. We instinctively recognize it. But analyzing our own depression can prove difficult. We need to view ourselves as logically as possible, but that proves difficult when our emotions are in turmoil. Outside help, sympathy, and understanding help us deal with depression.

Sleep Patterns Change
The depressed person rarely sleeps normally. His usual patterns of rest change in direct relation to his depression. He has trouble falling asleep. He awakens in the middle of the night and can't get back to sleep, or he awakens extremely early. In a few instances the depressed person sleeps far longer than necessary.

The depressed person finds that long, sleepless periods make him desperate. He tosses and turns, rearranges the covers, tries to relax, counts sheep, but nothing works. Sleeping pills often seem an attractive aid, but are not effective in the long term.

Appetite Diminishes

- "I'm not hungry."
- "Nothing tastes good."
- "I don't care for anything right now."
- "I don't feel well. I can't eat."

Depression is a sickening feeling that allows no interest in food. Of course, depressed people need proper nutrition as an integral part of their recovery, but food lacks appeal. They already feel dreadful and the thought of eating leaves them cold. Weight loss comes quickly to a depressed person.

Only occasionally does a seriously depressed person overeat. But when it does happen and the extra poundage rolls on, the depression increases.

Sexual Interest Wanes

Along with depression comes a marked loss of interest in sexual activity. Depression turns thoughts inward and it becomes very difficult to concentrate on the needs of another. Unless the depressed person's partner maintains a considerate and compassionate attitude, conflict will inevitably result.

Crying Is Frequent

"I can't help crying. I don't have any reason to cry, I just start and I can't stop. Sometimes it happens when I'm at work.

Depressed people vent their emotions by crying.

Usually they haven't a clue as to the basic cause for the depression. They only know they can't restrain their tears. "Don't cry. There's nothing to cry about," they are often told. Such advice makes them feel even more inadequate because they can't control themselves. They search desperately for a way to avoid crying. They try smiling instead, but smiles masking tears aren't very convincing.

Physical Appearance Suffers

The depressed person looks depressed. The shoulders sag. The head is down. Movements are slow. After all, why stand tall and rush around? Nothing is worth all that effort. The burden of depression weighs so heavily that it's impossible to straighten up and move briskly.

Vague aches and pains, a sad countenance, and lethargy all combine to define the appearance of a depressed person.

Behavior Is Unpredictable

In their frantic attempts to escape the clutches of depression, people behave unpredictably. Outgoing, sociable people become withdrawn, quiet, and moody. Normally reticent people talk loudly and become hostile, and aggressive. Depressed people have difficulty making decisions. They spend money unwisely. They watch too many movies. They may work hard one day and sit around the next.

Depressed people do not want to behave unpredictably. It is simply part of the pattern of life brought about by depression.

Thinking Is Negative

Depressed people experience painful, pessimistic thoughts. They brood over their condition. They feel sad, helpless, unloved, and lonely. They are convinced they are worthless, and no use to anyone. They feel boxed in, trapped by their dejection, melancholy, and despondent. They don't like what they are thinking, but when they attempt to redirect their thoughts, cheerfulness lasts only momentarily or never appears at all.

A depressed person's speech reflects these thoughts:

- "I'm no good."
- "I'm no use to anyone."
- "I've never done anything right in my whole life and it's too late to change."
- "No one wants me around."

One of the most significant needs in the life of a depressed person is to have help in changing these negative thought patterns.

Delusions Replace Reality

Depression may become so severe that a person becomes deluded. They may imagine things that have never happened, or that are not happening. When a person reaches this state, he needs professional help quickly. A deluded person can't be reached by reason and argument. Expert care must be found.

How to Handle Depression

Perhaps the most difficult part of depression is the slowness of recovery. Because the symptoms are so painful, the depressed person longs for quick relief. He craves permanent freedom from the persistent mental pain and misery he feels.

Remember that we aren't talking about the blues that last a day or two, or a week of discouragement, but weeks and months of painful, aching misery.

Renewal takes time and effort. Setbacks often occur. Depression doesn't heal overnight. But anyone who has experienced depression and recovery knows the sweet feeling of stable emotional health.

When depression lingers for more than two weeks, or if it intensifies progressively, there are some practical steps to take which should help.

See Your Doctor

The depression may have a physical cause and could be corrected by medical treatment. However, this is not common. A physician may be able to suggest additional help, perhaps some light sedative to aid sleeping, or calm anxious thoughts. You may receive help in determining a nutritious diet, or possibly in finding the cause of the depression.

The symptoms of depression bring such acute distress that the sufferer is soon convinced that it is certainly serious, maybe even fatal. A sympathetic explanation from a physician alleviates much useless worry.

Certainly it is comforting to be examined and receive the reassurance that the tightness in your chest comes from the tension of depression—not from a failing heart—and that your headaches and insomnia too, are a common symptom of depression. It is helpful to hear that your tears will not fall forever, but will stop when your depression lifts.

Don't be ashamed or hesitant to tell your doctor of all your symptoms and failings. He has heard them all before, and won't be shocked or disgusted. He needs the truth if he is to help you.

Maintain a Relationship with God

"I don't feel like reading the Bible. I can't pray. I feel so terrible. I know I should, but I just can't concentrate." A fifty-year-old Christian made this statement after several months of damaging depression. After talking with her briefly, we found she was trying to absorb Scripture in large portions and trying to spend extended time in prayer.

One side effect of depression is the inability to concentrate, a lack of specific focus. Therefore, any spiritual intake must be in small amounts—several times a day, a few verses of Scripture from the Psalms perhaps, followed by brief times of prayer. It is vital to allow the healing power of the word of God to wash over your life frequently. We recommend reading the Psalms or the Gospels whenever depressed.

Confess any known sin and accept God's forgiveness. Be careful, however, that the weight of depression doesn't lead you into a morbid review of all your past mistakes and sins, or a desperate, stream of confession that you hope will please God.

Try to Maintain a Thankful Spirit

"Give thanks in all circumstances" (1 Thessalonians 5:18). Maybe you feel you have nothing to be thankful for. Life is meaningless, you're miserable, hope doesn't exist. But if you know Christ as Savior, you can give thanks that your name is written in heaven. In obedience to God, not in response to feelings, we thank God consistently.

Rely On the Holy Spirit

Remember that God has given us the Holy Spirit who functions as our Comforter and Counselor. "And I will ask the Father, and he will give you another Counselor to be with you forever (John 14:16).

Praise be to the God and Father of our Lord Jesus Christ, the Father of compassion and the God of all comfort, who comforts us in all our troubles, so that we can comfort those in any trouble with the comfort we ourselves have received from God (2 Corinthians 1:3-4).

God provides a purpose and the balm for the experience of depression when he tells us in these passages that he will give us comfort and eventually will use this experience for good. "The richest lives with the fullest joys are those who have also tasted deeply of grief, sorrow and testing. Jesus was called 'a man of sorrows and acquainted with grief.'"[3]

Discipline Your Mind to Be Hopeful

Reject any thoughts of self-condemnation and embarrassment. Accept the reality of your depression but focus on the future when you will be well again. Imagine yourself whole and happy. Visualize yourself climbing out of the depression and functioning normally again. Such an exercise proves difficult but the benefits of such positive thinking can occur quickly.

Take Care of Your Body

You may need help if your depression is so acute that you don't care what happens to you.

Try to eat nutritious foods in small amounts several times during the day. Avoid junk foods that contribute nothing to your health. Take a stress vitamin daily.

Get adequate rest. You may need the help of sleeping pills for a time to get the rest essential to your recovery.

Even though you may not care about your appearance, force yourself to stay well groomed. That alone will lift your spirits, for even though inwardly you are suffering, you will still present a pleasing appearance.

Listen to Music
If you are at home during the day, listen to soothing Christian music. Avoid agitating or raucous music that will strain your nerves.

Find a Place to Contribute
Dr. Karl Menninger, the famous psychiatrist, was answering questions from the audience after giving a lecture on mental health.

"What would you advise a person to do," asked one man, "if that person felt a nervous breakdown coming on?"

Most people expected him to reply, "Consult a psychiatrist." To their astonishment, he replied, "Lock up your house, go across the railway tracks, find someone in need and do something to help that person."[4]

Reach out to someone, even in a minor way. This is, in a sense, bootstrap therapy. Pick yourself up and extend yourself to someone whose need is greater than yours. What can you do? Keep it simple and small to begin with. Depressed people often get that way because they overextended themselves in the first place. So take on a small task that allows you to give yourself to another.

- Write a short note to someone you know who is lonely.
- Volunteer to help in your church nursery once a month. You too, men. Children accept you as you are, depression and all.
- Take an elderly person for a drive.
- In some small way, lift the load of a family member.

Don't expect or look for appreciation. You are helping yourself by helping others.

Seek Counsel

Maybe you have done all you can and still your depression worsens. You have struggled, but nothing changed. Don't hesitate to seek help. Approach a family member or trusted friend first. Then, if they can't give the constructive, objective help you need, look for further help. See your pastor, a Christian counselor, or a Christian psychiatrist. Finances may discourage you from seeking professional help, but an expenditure now is an investment in your future.

We strongly recommend receiving help from a Christian, one who will counsel and help you on the basis of biblical principles and guidelines. Lasting help comes from the word of God. "But his delight is in the law of the Lord, and on his law he meditates day and night. He is like a tree planted by streams of water, which yields its fruit in season and whose leaf does not wither. Whatever he does prospers" (Psalm 1:2-3).

How to Help a Depressed Person

When we are close to a depressed person, we have an opportunity to help in a significant way. But we need to remember that alone we cannot effect a recovery. If we try to take full responsibility for the recovery, we open ourselves to a weight of unwarranted responsibility and the guilt of failure.

Perhaps your usually cheerful mate has slidden into a depression. Don't presume that something you have done has triggered the depression and your presence and attitude only worsens their problem. This is usually not true. Don't demand explanations or reasons for the depression. Often depressed people don't understand it themselves.

Perhaps something you did in the past contributed to the depression, but if you have asked forgiveness, drop the subject. A constant rehash of the problem won't lift the depression. Logic and argument only confuse and bewilder.

Be Sympathetic and Understanding

Consider Proverbs 31:26. "She speaks with wisdom, and faithful instruction is on her tongue." When dealing with depressed people, it's necessary to exercise wisdom, sympathy, and kindness. But draw the line on offering pity. They need positive direction, someone who will focus their thinking on recovery and the future. Too much pity keeps their thoughts glued to their present suffering.

Guard against being too cheerful in the presence of depressed people. "Like one who takes away a garment on a cold day, or like vinegar poured on soda, is one who sings songs to a heavy heart" (Proverbs 25:20).

Limit your expectations for interaction. Sometimes silent company works well. It assures the depressed one that you appreciate their presence. They are worthwhile, their mere presence is enough to satisfy. Don't be perturbed by their tears.

Offer Creative Alternatives

Often depressed people cannot motivate themselves to make a move toward recovery, even though they know what should be done. Gently suggest possibilities. Brusque commands won't gain any response, so maintain a consistent, gentle approach.

This attitude will take the grace of God, for often a

depressed person will show little response or appreciation.

Let Ephesians 4:32 be the basis of your relationship, "Be kind and compassionate to one another, forgiving each other, just as in Christ God forgave you."

Kindness may meet with indifference, but it communicates care and concern and eventually provides a basis of support on which the depressed person can begin to rebuild his self-image.

Help Them to Function

Try to be certain the depressed person eats properly.

Suggest taking a walk or a ride in the car. Listen to music together. But if the response is negative, don't force the issue.

Some counselors recommend a pet for a depressed person. The care and attention a pet demands will give that person an outward focus. Animals give unreserved devotion. They don't judge emotions, they never evaluate the reasons for tears and they don't insist on proper interactive responses.

Offer Genuine Commendation

Encourage and commend the depressed person. Don't be gushy or condescending. Depression does not lower a person's intelligence. They are more keenly aware of insincerity at this point in their life. Whenever it is possible, give genuine encouragement, for this will assist their recovery.

Use the Word of God and Prayer

If they seem indifferent to spiritual activity, read short passages of the Bible to them.

One woman told us that one of the most helpful aspects of her recovery took place several times a week. A

Christian friend would come to her home, speak a few words of encouragement, read the Bible briefly, kneel by her bed, hold her hands and pray for her recovery. This Christian friend never dwelt on the depression, never allowed critical remarks to pass her lips, and always encouraged her friend with the word of God.

Do not allow your mid-life opportunities and joys to be spoiled by depression and its accompanying traumas. Begin now to get back on top emotionally and spiritually. You can do it with God's help.

NOTES: 1. Frederick W. Ilfeld, Jr., M.D., "Current Social Stressors and Symptoms of Depression," *American Journal of Psychiatry,* vol. 134, no. 2, February, 1977, page 165.
2. Tim LaHaye, *How to Win Over Depression* (Grand Rapids, Michigan: Zondervan Publishing House, 1974), page 88.
3. Ruth Myers, "How to Cope with Depression," *NAVLOG* (Colorado Springs, Colorado: July, 1979), page 3.
4. Dr. Karl Menninger, in *Bits and Pieces* (Fairfield, New Jersey: Economics Press, June, 1976), page 5.

CHAPTER 6

Building and Rebuilding

Building Life Reserves

It is not unusual to press ourself beyond our normal limits in many areas of life. For instance, most people can get by on only a few hours of sleep for two or three days, if they are well-rested at the beginning. However, if they are already tired, two or three days of little sleep would be almost unbearable and could make them ill.

Several years ago a close friend, Mert Martin, shared a helpful illustration on building life reserves. Here is a modified version of the illustration.

We all have three major areas of life—physical, emotional, and spiritual. In each of these areas we build up reserves for times of unusual need. Consider first the physical. Imagine your physical being as a bucket. (See Figure 6-1).

When we live from day to day, we burn our physical energy down to the reserve level. Then we replenish with food, rest, and exercise. Occasionally we dip into the reserves and use more energy than we do normally. It then takes longer to replenish our energy reserve.

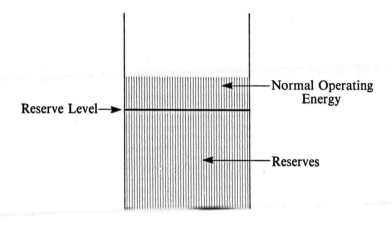

Figure 6-1

But suppose the reserve level is as shown in Figure 6-2.

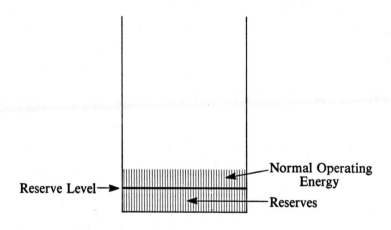

Figure 6-2

Now there is little or no reserve of physical energy to call upon in times of stress. The outcome is physical exhaustion or illness which necessitates a rebuilding process.

Now picture all three areas as in Figure 6-3.

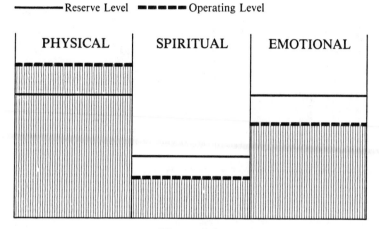

Figure 6-3

These three areas comprise our total self. We can operate in several ways.

- Above the reserve level in all areas
- Above the reserve level in one area and below in the others, as shown
- Below the reserve level in all areas
- And a variety of additional combinations

In each area we can dip below the normal reserve level. When a reserve is exhausted, or low, we experience illness (physical), sin (spiritual), and nervous breakdowns (emotional).

This is still not an accurate picture of a Christian's life. For God is the source of every area of our life—the physical and emotional as well as the spiritual. God "has given us everything we need for *life* and godliness" (2 Peter 1:3). "My God will meet *all* your needs" (Philippians 4:19). "Seek first his kingdom and his righteousness, and *all* these things will be given to you as well" (Matthew 6:33). Therefore, a more accurate picture of life would be as shown in Figure 6-4.

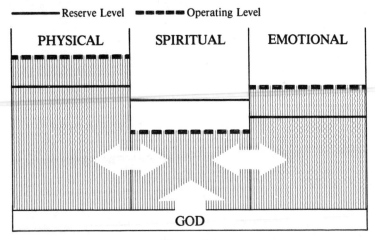

Figure 6-4

Think of the reserve areas as a savings account. They can either be exhausted or drawn upon in times of need. The three areas exhibit a certain independence and interdependence. *The spiritual area feeds the other two in a primary way.* Of course, our physical and emotional reserves also affect our spiritual intake. Exhausting resources in any area will cripple the Christian's effectiveness. Try drawing a similar picture of your life as you see it today.

The next three sections of this chapter give some practical suggestions on building our physical, emotional, and spiritual reserves.

Building Spiritual Reserves

Spiritual reserves provide the foundation for both the physical and emotional areas. They are interdependent, but for the Christian, spiritual reserves give the strength that non-Christians cannot tap.

The primary foundation is Jesus Christ. "For no one can lay any foundation other than the one already laid, which is Jesus Christ" (1 Corinthians 3:11). Being religious is not sufficient. The only sure foundation is knowing Christ as our personal Savior experiencing a spiritual rebirth followed by a living relationship with Christ.

"But each one should be careful how he builds (upon the foundation)" (1 Corinthians 3:10). Watch how a master craftsman carefully prepares his materials. He knows which tools to employ. Then he builds carefully, taking time and exercising patience, until he finishes.

Some years ago Roger Brandt, a close friend and fellow faculty member of the United States Air Force Academy, helped me build some bookshelves. I thought we would slap them together in an evening or two. After all, I had sketched out the plans so all we had to do was build them. Roger carefully selected and measured the boards. After several checks he finally cut them to length while I tried to be useful by holding the ends or catching scraps.

Now, I thought, we'll quickly nail them together and be done. But first he grooved the boards to insert the shelves and dividers. Then he used the router to round the edges. Then he re-checked each measurement. Several times he carefully put everything together and then took it apart again to make small adjustments.

The shelves were finally glued (not nailed) and set up. Now to throw on some stain and finish it, I thought. But it was not quite that simple. Roger patiently finished the shelving into a quality piece of furniture. It took almost two weeks, but the shelves still stand in my office, after being installed in three homes, and they reflect the quality of the craftsmanship that built them.

I was impatient. I wanted the bookshelves to progress from an idea to reality with little or no effort. Similarly, in the Christian life we want to grow fast. But building spiritual reserves and growing in Christ takes time and perseverance. If you build shabbily, your life almost certainly will collapse when you reach mid-life.

Many Christians go through years of Christian activity reaping spiritual truth vicariously though others. But they have not built their own personal lives on the Scriptures. In times of stress, borrowed truth is like beautifully displayed imitation food behind glass—beautiful to look at, pleasant to remember, but inaccessible and useless. In the midst of stress we are frequently unwilling to build and rebuild our foundations.

There are several indispensable tools for building the Christian life.

1. *A daily time of Bible reading and prayer.* I listed all my spiritual activities to determine the one most basic aspect of Christian growth which I would keep going at all costs. It is my daily devotional time of reading the Scriptures and praying. It is the simplest, most necessary activity to keep me going as a Christian. This daily time of personal devotions need not be lengthy or complicated—just regular.

   The first element of the quiet time is Scripture. Begin in the New Testament and read small portions such as a few verses or a chapter. As you read, meditate on it and pray about how it applies to your life.[1]

   Then spend a few minutes in prayer. Thank God

for what he has done for you. Share your burdens with him. Pray for your family, friends, and relatives. Many people find it helpful to keep a list of personal needs and prayer requests from others to help them pray more effectively and to record God's answers.

Regularity makes the quiet time with God a strengthening and stabilizing influence in your life. Pick a time available on a daily basis. As little as 15 minutes each day amounts to 75 hours a year (over nine full work days!) if you do it only 300 days in that year.

Can you imagine the influence this private time with God could have on your life and outlook? This time must be a priority or it slips away. It is helpful to take time to read the Scriptures *before* eating breakfast, watching television, reading a book or newspaper, or working. Once you have started the habit, you will look forward to it daily as a special time. Make a realistic goal meeting with God on five out of six days a week, one of which should be on the weekend when you can make it a more leisurely time.[2]

2. *Personal Bible study.* "For many years Monterey, a California coast town, was a pelican's paradise. As the fishermen cleaned their fish they flung the offal to the pelicans. The birds grew fat, lazy and contented. Eventually, however, the offal was utilized commercially and there were no snacks for the pelicans.

"When the change came the pelicans made no effort to fish for themselves. They waited around, grew gaunt and thin. Many starved to death. They had forgotten how to fish for themselves. The problem was solved by importing pelicans from the south, birds accustomed to foraging for themselves. They were placed among their starving cousins, and the newcomers immediately started catching fish. Before long the hungry pelicans followed suit and the famine was ended."[3]

This describes many of us. We become so used to letting others feed us spiritually that we forget how to forage in God's word for ourself.

The word "study" frightens many of us. We do not think of ourselves as students. Yet, we study all the time. We study how to do a particular task at work. We buy books on auto repair, stereo systems, new appliances, hobbies, sports, and a host of other subjects, to learn how to do something.

When we know what the Bible teaches, we build a key reserve for coping with mid-life crises. Second-hand knowledge of the Bible leaves us feeling empty and undernourished. "Do your best to present yourself to God as one approved, a workman who does not need to be ashamed and who correctly handles the word of truth" (2 Timothy 2:15).

You may feel that reading the Bible is hard enough without studying it too. But Bible study is really quite simple. Here are some easy suggestions:

- Use a personal study guide (such as the "Design for Discipleship" Bible study series available from The Navigators), or studies on particular books of the Bible which can be found in any Christian bookstore.
- Meet with a small group. Bible study is difficult (though not impossible) to do alone. We need the stimulation of a small group where we are accountable to prepare and share regularly.
- Prepare ahead of time. You will receive in proportion to what you put into the study.

Sermons and Sunday school classes, though excellent input, rarely meet the need for concentrated Bible study, because hearing is the only sense used. Study involves input through your eyes, into your mind, and onto paper.

To find a study group, check with your church or ask a more mature Christian to start one. Perhaps you could start one yourself.[4]

3. *Fellowship.* "Misery loves company," is an old saying. In the midst of any crisis, we need others to empathize and to help. Mutual sharing and help is what Christian fellowship is all about. "Two are better than one, because they have a good return for their work. If one falls down, his friend can help him up! But pity the man who falls and has no one to help him up!" (Ecclesiastes 4:9-10). "And let us consider how we may spur one another on toward love and good deeds. Let us not give up meeting together, as some are in the habit of doing, but let us encourage one another—and all the more as you see the Day approaching" (Hebrews 10:24-25).

When a crisis hits—especially a mid-life crisis—our first move may be toward isolation. We are embarrassed and confused, so we withdraw. But we desperately need fellowship and friendship at such a time. You may argue that church services with everyone dressed neatly, singing, listening and reciting in unison are a far cry from fellowship. But you can meet other Christians there and find out about small groups where *personal* fellowship thrives. If you already fellowship with other believers, don't quit when a crisis comes for that's when you need it most.

Building Physical Reserves
"Everyone who competes in the games goes into strict

training. . . .I beat my body and make it my slave" (1 Corinthians 9:25 and 27). God expects us to be good stewards of all he has given, including our body.

No one needs to begin jogging six miles a day or to become a health food fanatic. We simply need to use common sense and a moderate amount of self-discipline.

1. *Eating habits.* Americans (including Christians) consume far more food than a population twice our number needs. Yet, we are not necessarily in good physical health. Overeating, junk foods, and unbalanced diets characterize the habits of many people.

   For weight control, push-aways from the table provide the simplest answer, but require much self discipline. If you learn and practice sensible nutrition, you will feel much better physically.

2. *Physical exercise.* Shortness of breath, tiredness, and back trouble are only a few of the symptoms of inadequate physical exercise. Even one who looks trim may simply have a higher metabolism and stay thinner without being physically fit. Regular physical exercise will not only make you feel better and possibly lengthen your life, but it can give you a new view of yourself and a new outlook on life.

   Until two years ago Mary had no regular exercise. She is not athletic, so only participated reluctantly in sports. Then she began to jog at the age of forty. It literally changed her outlook on life. She developed greater stamina, a more competitive spirit, and larger emotional capacity.

   Walking, jogging, raquetball, tennis, running and basic calisthenics are all possibilities.[5] If you have any question about your ability to exercise strenuously, be sure to consult your physician. Start slowly, but above all, start and keep it up long enough to enjoy the benefits.

3. *Physical examinations.* A friend of ours on Navigator staff, Cecil Davidson, entered his sixties actively leading a ministry to servicemen. After some prodding he had a physical check-up and emerged with a bill of perfect health. The doctor asked what he did to keep in shape. "I play football every Saturday with the servicemen!" he replied.

You may not be quite so active, though you still may feel you are in perfect health. But, feelings can deceive. You need a periodic check-up. Your life may depend on it. Physical problems detected early can often be treated, whereas later in life a cure may be hopeless. We suggest a physical once a year, or at least once every two years, after age thirty-five. A medical examination is expensive, but it is money well spent. It's your life, which is infinitely priceless.

4. *Rest.* Regular, effective rest and sleep undergird our entire physical and emotional well-being. Try to determine the right amount of sleep for you and discipline yourself to get it.

Most people require between six and nine hours of sleep. Regularity is as important as the amount. In mid-life, controlled rest becomes more important because burning the candle at both ends is a sure way of igniting a mid-life crisis.

Building Emotional Reserves

A physical exam tells you the condition of your body. But where do we get an emotional examination? Usually we don't even consider our emotional needs until we approach a nervous breakdown. Emotional evaluations do exist in very limited form and accuracy. They are only indicators at best. One that is readily available is the Taylor-Johnson Temperament Analysis Test. Many pastors and counselors are trained to administer and interpret it. We encourage you to try it to gain some insight into yourself. We took it and found it was very useful.

Emotional repairs are time consuming and stressful. It is much better to build deep emotional reserves rather than to repair and rebuild. Here we will identify a few key areas that can either build or deplete our emotional resources.

1. *The marriage relationship.* Some of life's most rewarding relationships take place in marriage. When those relationships are good, they give emotional support and replenishment beyond description. When they are bad, they sap every ounce of the emotional reserves we possess. In mid-life the frills and flowers of marriage begin to fall away, exposing the marriage to full examination by both husband and wife. With the additional stress of teenagers and career, we must exert extra care in building the marriage relationship.

2. *Job and career.* Marriage and career fight for dominance in the lives of most men, and an increasing number of women. A positive view of work and career gives great emotional stability. Many emotional resources are expended needlessly at work over matters of very little importance. How to fit work into life and family is a major task of mid-life.[9]

3. *Children.* In the early years of marriage, children drain us physically. In mid-life they drain or build us emotionally. Chapter 8 is on teenagers, tagalongs, and grandchildren.

4. *Recreation.* In times of stress, diversions and recreation rebuild our emotional resources. Many Christians are so busy with jobs, families, and church that they

neglect refreshing recreation. Many families choose recreation that conflicts with church activities or that is more work than rest, which drains, instead of building. We need regular recreational activities interspersed among stressful activities. Some ideas are:

- Reading
- Hobbies in the home
- Sports
- Music
- Taking a college course
- Watching a *specific* weekly television show
- Knitting
- Photography
- Hiking
- Gardening
- Crafts

Recreation need not be expensive. It need only be different from your required tasks—something you select that brings you pleasure. Its purpose is to re-create your emotions. But recreation does not just happen; it needs to be planned. It will take time, but it is time well spent and will pay dividends for years to come.

5. *Specific emotional drains.* Many incidents and circumstances drain us emotionally and create special problems. Each of us can list these almost without thinking. In mid-life we need to reduce them or learn to handle them better. Some of them are:

- Unresolved conflicts
- Suspicion of others' motives
- Overscheduling and overactivity

The list of key areas could go beyond these five. Our emotional reserves must be built and protected. They are not manufactured automatically. Many other things help build this reserve bank.

- A strong spiritual walk
- Confidence that God is in charge of your life
- Rest and exercise. Physical and emotional health are closely linked.
- A good personal self-image
- A few deep personal relationships

Key Biblical Concepts

The incidents which produce mid-life crises are not the roots of those crises. Their basic cause is an inadequate understanding of God's character and purposes. The primary cures are found by developing one's understanding of God and basing one's life on a strong relationship with him.

Certain key biblical concepts and doctrines underlie the teaching of this book and the proper response to a mid-life crisis. Without Bible-based concepts we tend to wallow about in the morass of our feelings and emotions, never planting our feet on solid ground. Most of these concepts concern our view of God and how he acts in the world. They are theological issues of deep and far-reaching importance. These issues answer the questions:

- Is God still in charge?
- What have I done wrong?
- What is God doing to me?
- Is it too late to get right with God?

One who can respond properly to these four questions possesses the doctrinal foundation to survive any crisis, mid-life or otherwise.

The Sovereignty of God (Is God still in charge?)

For centuries theologians have studied, discussed, and written about the nature of God's sovereignty. No one has yet produced an answer which the human mind can easily grasp. The study becomes more complex as we try to explain man's free will versus God's sovereignty. Those concepts seem inextricably locked in opposition to one another. Yet, the fact of God's sovereignty is fundamental to all of life.

Webster defines sovereignty as "supreme power . . . freedom from external control . . . controlling influence."[7] Applied to God, this means he has total authority, power, and control over all creation. God is sovereign in all aspects of our personal life and in world events. Consider the following statements from Scripture as a summary of his sovereignty.

God is sovereign over nature. "For every animal of the forest is mine, and the cattle on a thousand hills. I know every bird in the mountains, and the creatures of the field are mine. If I were hungry I would not tell you, for the world is mine, and all that is in it" (Psalm 50:10-12). "The heavens are yours, and yours also the earth; you founded the world and all that is in it" (Psalm 89:11).

God is sovereign over rulers and governments. "O Lord, God of our fathers, are you not the God who is in heaven? You rule over all the kingdoms of the nations. Power and might are in your hand, and no one can withstand you" (2 Chronicles 20:6). "No one from the east or the west, or from the desert can exalt a man. But it is God who judges: He brings one down, he exalts another"

(Psalm 75:6,7). "The King's heart is in the hand of the Lord; he directs it like a watercourse wherever he pleases" (Proverbs 21:1).

God is sovereign over my personal circumstances. "And we know that in all things God works for the good of those who love him, who have been called according to his purpose" (Romans 8:28).

God is sovereign over my physical and emotional makeup.

> For you created my inmost being; you knit me together in my mother's womb. I praise you because I am fearfully and wonderfully made; your works are wonderful, I know that full well. My frame was not hidden from you when I was made in the secret place. When I was woven together in the depths of the earth, your eyes saw my unformed body. All the days ordained for me were written in your book before one of them came to be (Psalm 139:13-16).

But, if God is sovereign, can I make any free choices? Yes. God has all the powers of sovereign control, but yet allows us to make various choices. He knows what we will choose, and allows us to live with the results of our choices. Yet, he specifies certain limits or boundaries. He promises to control the external circumstances of our life for our good. We may not always view our circumstances favorably but he knows what will be for our perfect good. We then select our responses to the external circumstances that God allows.

Perhaps you feel that the truth of God's sovereignty and our ability to choose are diametrically opposed to each other. Yet, both are taught in Scripture. We accept them as facts of Scripture which the human mind cannot fully grasp. " 'For my thoughts are not your thoughts, neither are your ways my ways,' declares the Lord. 'As the heavens are higher than the earth, so are my ways higher than your ways, and my thoughts than your thoughts'" (Isaiah 55:8-9)

For example, the concept of gravity undergirds all space flight and all of human life on this planet. Yet, no one can explain gravity. No one understands where it comes from or what causes it. Yet, we describe it in equations, experience it, and are totally dependent on it for the sustenance of life. Not understanding gravity does not prevent us from recognizing it, living with it, and using it. Similarly, while we may not fully understand God's sovereignty, we can accept it and order our lives by it.

In addition to recognizing God's sovereignty, we must recognize that he *always* has our best interests at heart. "What, then, shall we say in response to this? If God is for us, who can be against us?" (Romans 8:31). "Are not two sparrows sold for a penny? Yet not one of them will fall to the ground apart from the will of your Father. And even the very hairs of your head are all numbered. So don't be afraid; you are worth more than many sparrows" (Matthew 10:29-31).

The combination of God's sovereignty and God's love provides a sturdy foundation for living in any circumstance. However, you can choose not to believe these truths. What are the practical results of *not* accepting God's sovereignty and love?

1. *Fear* that God is not in control and cannot or will not protect and help you.
2. *Rebellion*, thinking that God is not in control so you can oppose and overrule his ultimate purposes for your life.

3. *Bitterness* against God for his seeming inability to protect you and control your circumstances.
4. *Fighting* God for control of your circumstances, assuming that you can escape or control them.
5. *Uncertainty* about God's purpose or seeming capriciousness in the daily affairs of your life.
6. *Doubting* God's concern and love for you.

Any one of these attitudes leads to spiritual dryness and a questioning of God's love, motives, and wisdom.

On the other hand, accepting God's sovereignty and love for us results in a completely different outlook on life:

1. *Peace*, knowing that God is in control and guarding your best interests.
2. *Rest,* knowing you do not need to struggle against God or your circumstances to survive.
3. *Confidence* in God's power to work on your behalf.
4. *Faith* in God which grows through the process of seeing God develop the circumstances in your life for your ultimate good.
5. *Optimism*, knowing that the final outcome and victory are assured.

God remains sovereign whether we believe it or not. The truth of God's sovereignty can be stated briefly and simply, but is so deep and far-reaching that you may want to study this doctrine in much greater depth.[8]

Acceptance of God's sovereignty provides the proper perspective with which we should approach any mid-life crisis. In light of his sovereignty we understand several things:

1. God made you with a physical makeup that experi-

ences constant change, development, and decay. A normal part of being human is experiencing the physical realignment of mid-life.

2. God made you an emotional being with certain personality characteristics, strengths, and weaknesses. The very emotional responses and reactions of mid-life provide the basis for God to intervene in your life in a new, fresh way.

3. Even when many incidents of your past resulted from sin and bad choices, God will now use these lessons to rebuild and mature you from now on. The history of your marriage (or singleness), career, and personal accomplishments are under God's sovereign control and will fit his purposes for your future.

4. Whatever your current emotional struggles or problems, God will take you through them and make you into a more mature and happier person. There is *always* light at the end of the tunnel.

5. In the context of God's sovereignty, you still retain the right of choice, but you must live with the results. "Do not be deceived: God cannot be mocked. A man reaps what he sows" (Galatians 6:7). God *knows* what we will choose. God *could* ordain or determine what we choose, but he does not do so. "Whoever has my commands and obeys them, he is the one who loves me. He who loves me shall be loved by my Father, and I too will love him and show myself to him" (John 14:21).

Grace Versus Works (What have I done wrong?)
Any time we face problems we suspect that we have sinned and God is punishing us. Upon investigation we usually find many areas of our lives that God could justly condemn. Then we begin a process of self-condemnation

and an attempt at self-reformation. But such a process, though perhaps needed, strikes at the wrong source.

In mid-life our past is unchangeable, and an analysis of past sin can pre-occupy our minds. We begin doubting the reality of our relationship with God. God fades in our troubled minds as a viable resource and help. We think of him punishing us instead of helping us.

An understanding of grace and works can be a key factor in reversing the downward spiral. It is relatively easy to believe that we are saved by grace. Our relationship with God is based upon grace and finds expression in the teaching of justification.

> He saved us, not because of righteous things we had done, but because of his mercy. He saved us through the washing of rebirth and renewal by the Holy Spirit, whom he poured out on us generously through Jesus Christ our Savior, so that having been justified by his grace, we might become heirs having the hope of eternal life (Titus 3:5-7).

After salvation most of us tend to build our relationship with God on what we do, such as attend church, share our faith, do Bible study or help the poor. We labor diligently. We struggle against sin. We try to change our habits. We even study key doctrines of justification, salvation, and sanctification. We become doers to such an extent that our relationship with God settles into a series of disciplines, activities, and works. They are good and give great personal satisfaction. We *feel* we are doing something *for* God. But subtly we transfer from dependence on God to dependence on our works and suddenly find ourselves devoid of grace.

Then if a mid-life crisis descends, we experience a

mixed onslaught of feelings; the works no longer satisfy because we have a renewed desire to do something lasting with our lives—something more than occasional good works. We feel guilty and a new lack of spiritual motivation, and desire creeps in. It is precisely at this time that we must return to the basics of our relationship with God. We were saved by grace through faith. "For it is by grace you have been saved, through faith—this is not from yourselves, it is the gift of God—not by works, so that no one can boast" (Ephesians 2:8-9).

We cannot work our way into salvation. Nor can we work ourselves out of a spiritual slump.

> So then just as you received Christ Jesus as Lord, continue to live in him, rooted and built up in him, strengthened in the faith, as you were taught, and overflowing with thankfulness. See to it that no one takes you captive through hollow and deceptive philosophy, which depends on human tradition and the basic principles of this world rather than on Christ. For in Christ all the fullness of the Deity lives in bodily form, and you have been given fullness in Christ, who is the head over every power and authority (Colossians 2:6-10).

We are to walk or live the Christian life in the same way that we received Jesus Christ. How was that? By grace through faith. Look at this passage carefully. We have already been rooted in the past, and God did the planting. The word "firmly," used in one translation, speaks of the security and completeness of the roots or planting. The other side of the coin is that we are *now* being built up by God. Verse 10 teaches that we are totally complete in Christ—lacking nothing.

In a crisis we must remember the basics of our relationship with God. No matter how we feel, we are still his child and he has not abandoned us. We only deepen our feelings of anxiety and inadequacy when we desperately grasp at works and activities to secure our standing with God. A return to a position of total dependence on him is necessary to reinstill our confidence and sense of security.

Spiritual Maturity (What is God doing to me?)

Blaming God for our problems and afflictions is as old as sin itself. After all, isn't God sovereign? Couldn't he have prevented this? He must be out to get me. When such thoughts flash through our minds we almost believe them because of their frequent recurrence.

God's purposes are far deeper than giving out petty punishments for our frequent misdeeds. He wants solid maturity in the life of a believer. The immature bristle with doubt in affliction, while the mature grow and deepen. A foundation of spiritual maturity carries us through *any* crisis.

But what is spiritual maturity? As we examine key passages of Scripture several characteristics stand out.

The spiritually mature person is:

1. *Teachable.* He is willing to learn, no matter what the cost. Teachability and humility are twins in practice. "Let the wise listen and add to their learning, and let the discerning get guidance" (Proverbs 1:5). See Proverbs 9:8-10 also. In a crisis the mature Christian becomes a learner, one who seeks and listens to wise counsel.
2. *Sound in doctrine and deep in God's word.* "Since an overseer is entrusted with God's work, he must be blameless. . .He must hold firmly to the trustworthy

message as it has been taught, so that he can encourage others by sound doctrine and refute those
who oppose it'' (Titus 1:7-9).

A person who knows the Scriptures and who
practices them has roots that will hold fast in any
storm. Their soundness and depth is not theoretical,
but practical. He does not merely possess head knowledge, but life knowledge. His doctrine and knowledge were formed in the forge fires of life. A mature
Christian prepares for crisis by developing depth in
the Scriptures. Crises, strong feelings, and struggles
will still come but *there will be roots* when you need
them.

3. *Patient—exhibiting self-control.* "An overseer. . .
must be . . . self-controlled" (Titus 1:7-8). Impulsiveness and anger in a crisis pave the way to defeat.
On the other hand, self-control and patience force
your mind and actions back to God and the Bible
which give victory. "But those who hope in the Lord
will renew their strength. They will soar on wings like
eagles; they will run and not grow weary, they will
walk and not be faint" (Isaiah 40:31).

4. *A man or woman of faith.* "And without faith it is
impossible to please God, because anyone who comes
to him must believe that he exists and that he rewards
those who earnestly seek him" (Hebrews 11:6). "Now
faith is being sure of what we hope for and certain of
what we do not see" (Hebrews 11:1). The mature
Christian possesses tested faith. It is faith experienced
in answered prayer, patiently waiting for God to
work, obeying God's will, and seeing God's promises
fulfilled.

5. *Sensible.* "The overseer must be . . . hospitable, loving what is good, sensible, . . ." (Titus 1:8 NASB). Sen-

sible means having good sense or using your head. God gave us a mind and wants us to use it under the direction of the Holy Spirit within the boundaries of Scripture. Clear thinking can rescue us from panic in the midst of a crisis. Impulsiveness and confused thinking will make us more unstable. We need to develop the habit of clear, Spirit-led thinking.

6. *Intent on pleasing God, not men.* Habitually measuring our actions by other's opinions and expectations weakens our ability to clearly discern God's will. "Whatever you do, work at it with all your heart, as working for the Lord, not for men, since you know that you will receive an inheritance from the Lord as a reward. It is the Lord Christ you are serving" (Colossians 3:23-24). It is God alone whom we serve, but we often guide our life by man's opinions. Man-pleasing is an ulcer-producing activity. Men are changeable, but God is not. He is constant and unchangeable. A mature Christian focuses on pleasing God, not men.

7. *Pursuing a holy life.* "But just as he who called you is holy, so be holy in all you do" (1 Peter 1:15). Holiness and Christlikeness are nearly the same. We need to be growing more and more into conformity with Jesus Christ in our thoughts, desires, and actions. Pursuing purity of life and holiness is no small thing. It is a lifelong goal. The constant pursuit of holiness and Christlikeness is a mark of a mature Christian.[10]

8. *Honest.* "Since an overseer is entrusted with God's work, he must be blameless" (Titus 1:7). An honest person possesses a reputation which no amount of power or position can buy. In a world where situation ethics rule everyday conduct, honesty is a rare com-

modity. Above all, it should be an obvious mark of a Christian. In the midst of a mid-life crisis, honesty with yourself and others as to what you are encountering will open new vistas of communication and help.''[11]

9. *Unselfish.* ''Do nothing out of selfish ambition or vain conceit'' (Philippians 2:3). Be ''not a lover of money'' (1 Timothy 3:3). Selfishness and materialism join hands to produce evidence of spiritual immaturity. The Bible says much on the topic of money and possessions, and our attitudes toward them. The mature Christian trusts God for his needs and selflessly gives himself to others without asking ''How much will this cost me?'' A focus on obtaining ''things'' —clothes, a stereo, furniture, a car, a home—blunts the inner desire to know God and serve others. Christ set the perfect example by giving himself fully and unselfishly on the cross for our sin to obtain our salvation. One may have been a Christian for many years and still be living selfishly with a materialistic outlook which tarnishes and hinders spiritual maturity. Learn to live for others, focusing on the eternal values they represent.

10. *Steadfast in hard times.* ''Therefore, my beloved brethren, be steadfast, immovable, always abounding in the work of the Lord, knowing that your toil is not in vain in the Lord'' (1 Corinthians 15:58 NASB). ''In this you greatly rejoice, though now for a little while, you may have had to suffer grief in all kinds of trials. These have come so that your faith—of greater worth than gold, which perishes, even though refined by fire—may be proved genuine and result in praise, glory and honor when Jesus Christ is revealed'' (1 Peter 1:6-7). A man or woman who endures difficult

times should grow in maturity and dependence on God. Deep roots do not develop in an easy chair during a soft life. They develop through trials and tests which drive us to depend on God.

Forgiveness and Restoration (Is it too late to get right with God?)

Many of us do not turn to God until we despair of any other help. Though it is unfortunate to wait so long, God still takes us in.

> Come to me, all you who are weary and burdened, and I will give you rest. Take my yoke upon you, and learn from me, for I am gentle and humble in heart, and you will find rest for your soul. For my yoke is easy, and my burden is light (Matthew 11:28-30).

No matter what you have done or are doing, forgiveness is at hand. Simply pray and confess your sin to God. He will restore you to fellowship and begin the process of building or rebuilding right now.

Rebuilding

The bottom may have just fallen out of your life and left you at a low ebb. Perhaps for the first time in your life you see no way out. You have nowhere to turn but to God.

Now God can take over and begin a rebuilding process. It is likely that much of your past life was built around your accomplishments and attempts to be happy and successful. But that is past. Now God has his chance, if you will give him the opportunity.

How can you rebuild? A few simple ideas follow:

Review Your Spiritual Foundation

Analyze your personal commitment to God. Give thanks for your salvation. If you discover you never really believed in Christ for salvation, do that now. In any event, recommit your life to God and ask for his help today in rebuilding your life.

Admit Your Present Need to God and Others

Honestly tell God how you feel and think. Find a Christian friend or counselor who will interact with you as you work through the issues of mid-life. Don't expect anyone to be an answer-man with all the solutions. God wants to teach *you* and help *you* understand and grow through your circumstances.

Be Willing to Start Over

To rebuild means to start over in many areas: your marriage, your spiritual life, your career, your self-esteem, your physical condition. Go back to the basics and build up some spiritual, physical, and emotional reserves as outlined earlier in this chapter. Re-anchor those moorings one at a time, remembering that it will take patience.

Set Goals

Insecurity and anxiety result naturally from wandering blindly with no certain destination. This is the time to set and clarify goals for your life. Begin with small goals to meet immediate needs. Then set goals for deeper and more far-reaching development.

And, whatever you do, don't quit! There are answers. This time will pass and you will either have developed spiritually or openly abandoned a walk with God. You must choose what happens. God is sufficient for your need now. He only wants you to turn to him in full dependence.

NOTES: 1. Many people use a devotional guide, such as *Our Daily Bread,* (available from Radio Bible Class, Box 22, Grand Rapids, Michigan 49555, free of charge), or *Streams in the Desert,* by Mrs. Charles E. Cowman (Grand Rapids, Michigan: Zondervan Publishing House, 1968).
2. *Appointment with God,* (Colorado Springs, Colorado: NavPress, 1973).
3. *Bits and Pieces* (Fairfield, New Jersey: Economics Press, June, 1976), page 23.
4. *Lead Out,* (Colorado Springs, Colorado: NavPress, 1975).
5. Kenneth H. Cooper, *Aerobics* (New York: Bantom Books, 1968).
6. Jerry and Mary White, *Your Job: Survival or Satisfaction?* (Grand Rapids, Michigan: Zondervan Publishing House, 1977).
7. *Webster's New Collegiate Dictionary* (Springfield, Massachusetts: G. & C. Merriam Company, 1973), page 1112.
8. Several excellent books for further study are available: J. I. Packer, *Knowing God* (Downers Grove, Illinois: Inter-Varsity Press, 1973); J. I. Packer, *Evangelism and the Sovereignty of God* (Downers Grove, Illinois: Inter-Varsity Press, n.d.); C. H. Spurgeon, *Spurgeon on the Attributes of God* (Tyndale Bible Society, Post Office Box 6006, MacDill AFB, Florida 33608); Edith Schaeffer, *Affliction* (Old Tappan, New Jersey: Fleming H. Revell, Co., 1975).
9. Dr. Joseph Cooke, *Free for the Taking,* (Old Tappan, New Jersey: Fleming H. Revell Co., 1975).
10. Jerry Bridges, *The Pursuit of Holiness* (Colorado Springs, Colorado: NavPress, 1978).
11. Jerry White, *Honesty, Morality, and Conscience* (Colorado Springs, Colorado: NavPress, 1978).

CHAPTER 7

Marriage in Mid-life

Late one afternoon Mike Russell came home from work. He asked his wife, Janice, to join him in their bedroom.

"Could it wait for a few minutes? Dinner is almost ready," she replied.

"No, it's important. Dinner can wait."

In the bedroom he simply announced, "Janice, I want a divorce. I've thought it all out. I've already rented an apartment and I'm leaving."

She sat in stunned silence, then stammered, "Mike, you're not serious, are you?" But the look on his face told her he was not kidding.

"Why? After so many years, why?" she stuttered.

"We'll talk more later. I've simply had it with the kids, your nagging, and hiding things from me, our relationship—the whole mess." He turned to leave.

"But, Mike, we're Christians. You know this isn't right," she pleaded.

"We've prayed, tried to change, and nothing has worked. I know what the Bible says, but I can't turn back. Christians or not, I've made up my mind." With that Mike packed, left and never returned to his family.

Twenty-three years of marriage, four children, deep involvement in spiritual things, and a mid-life career change in the midst of spiritual rebellion, all climaxed in this scene.

For most of their marriage Mike totally dominated the relationship. Janice acquiesced and became very quiet and submissive. Yet she began to undermine his authority with the children without really knowing what she was doing. Mike totally changed careers at age thirty-eight, but his new career floundered and gave no satisfaction. This, accompanied by spiritual rebellion, sent him into depression. Throughout this process their communication in every area of marriage deteriorated so they rarely discussed important issues or decisions.

In mid-life Mike and Janice repeated the patterns set early in their marriage. They failed to make needed changes after their early years together and reached a breaking point, a point of no return, which ultimately led to divorce. Could the disintegration of their marriage have been avoided? Yes. But how? That is the focus of this chapter—pinpointing some of the problems and discussing how to make marriage work during mid-life.

At the risk of oversimplification, Mike and Janice's marriage was the victim of:

1. A severe mid-life career change and crisis for Mike
2. Janice's inability to understand Mike's mid-life transition and their subsequent conflict over it
3. A severe spiritual depression for Mike when Janice became the family's spiritual leader
4. A communication breakdown over finances, teenagers, and spiritual matters at a time when Mike and Janice both had an acute need to be heard and understood

The same pattern is repeated hundreds of times with countless causes ranging from impatience to infidelity.

But let's not distort the situation. There are stories of increasingly happy marriages in mid-life. For many it is a time when marriage gets better and better.

Marriage in mid-life can vary from pure delight to tolerated misery. Marital conflicts become more subtle, but deeper. But in mid-life the potential for growth in our marriage dwarfs all past opportunities. In early mid-life we determine the degree of intimacy we will enjoy after our children have left home.

New dimensions in marriage come only when two people learn to know and understand each other in the climate of mid-life. Neither one is the same as when they married. They have each changed more than they realize. Moreover, they emerge with new expectations and new roles.

Changing Expectations and Roles

In mid-life we develop a new view of life. Our value systems change. We see things from a different perspective. We expect and desire different things from life in general than when we were younger. We expect different things of ourselves. We respond in a new way to circumstances and events.

Especially in marriage, we find our expectations and even our roles changing. This can be very disconcerting if the changes seem negative. It is even more confusing when husbands and wives change in varying ways and at different times. Let's examine some of the issues.

Indicators of a Marriage Crisis in Mid-life
Several indicators surface in mid-life which warn of

impending problems in marriage. When recognized, they can form the basis for significant growth and development.

A change in the sexual relationship is one of the most obvious indicators of a potential problem. When the frequency of sexual relations becomes a source of conflict, or if one partner's desire diminishes considerably, look for the root causes.

Staleness in marriage is quite common in mid-life. Husbands and wives begin taking each other for granted. The zip has left the relationship. When they are alone together, silence or indifference prevails. Romance is a thing of the past. This is especially crucial if you once experienced real vitality and enjoyment in being together. This staleness can easily make one partner look elsewhere for the fellowship and companionship that should come in the marriage.

Conflicts become more acute and cutting in mid-life marriage relationships. Our tolerance will either increase or decrease. As a multitude of mid-life changes affect the husband and wife, irritability increases. Conflicts become stronger and cut more deeply. They strike more at the dignity of the individual than at their actions. We apologize less frequently, leaving more and more issues unresolved. In fact, we may even conclude that he (or she) will never change, so why go through the hassle of discussion. When we observe this happening in our marriage we can be sure there are some deeper problems in our relationship which have not yet been solved.

Growing apart spiritually is a frightening occurrence. Yet, as goals change in mid-life, it is common for one partner to get turned on spiritually while the other lags far behind. He or she may even resent the partner's new-found spiritual enthusiasm. Even when both partners are growing spiritually, they can diverge if they find their primary fellowship and stimulation in separate groups. Do you discuss spiritual matters, especially those deeply personal to you? The ideal is a growing spiritual closeness in mid-life which sets the stage for years of ministry as a couple.

A focus on separate goals drives a wedge in any marriage. In the early years the financial struggle, the careers of husband and wife, and establishing a home almost automatically unify family goals. In mid-life, both partners begin to reevaluate their personal direction. As the children leave home, wives think more of a personal career or further education. Husbands may embark on a new mid-life career. The values of house, yard, recreation, free time, and money can change for both and drive them in opposite directions.

If you are developing significantly different goals from your spouse that are "yours" rather than "ours" guard against letting those goals pull you apart. In mid-life the tendency to selfishly "do what I want" often drowns a couple's unity. When one partner (often the husband) is so engrossed in an all-consuming goal, it can be so overpowering as to completely squash any of his partner's personal hopes or goals. We each need to form personal goals for growth. Frequently in mid-life the motivation for change is present, so it is a time to grow and change together while supporting one another in each other's goals.

In mid-life we become *more critical and quicker to voice disapproval*. There is an old saying; "Familiarity breeds contempt." Although this refers to authority relationships at work or in the military, it can also be true in marriage. Here, "Familiarity breeds contempt when not accompanied by love and commitment." When love and commitment diminish, we begin to see glaring faults in each other's appearance, personality, and character. Those faults were always there. We may even acknowledge that we saw them before. But now they have become grounds for criticism. Certain qualities begin to irritate—the tone of his voice, the disapproving way he wrinkles his face, the disparity between private and public means of talking, shape of her nose, the roll of fat around her waist, his unconcious mannerisms, and dozens of other minutiae which were of no consequence before. Now we see them, brood on them, and finally verbalize them to our spouse with hostility. Such criticisms are frequently voiced by a couple heading for divorce.

In past years couples would go through these various problems with tenacity and try to stay together even when they did not make great progress in resolving them. But in recent times, the divorce rate among Christians and non-Christians has soared, prompted by the idea that divorce presents an easy out. Couples today seem less tolerant of problems and more prone to quit. Mid-life is the second most vulnerable time for a divorce after the first two or three years of marriage.

Expectations and Expressions of Need

Many couples do not realize the contrast between their needs in their early twenties and during mid-life. Consider the following comparisons:

Young Couples	Mid-Life Couples
Idealistic.	Realistic.
Partners operate separately on the job and/or at home.	Both want support and understanding in their spheres of activity.
Tolerant of shortcomings.	Less tolerant of faults.

He encourages her independence.	He begins to resent her independence.
He tends to be the decision-maker.	He tends to abdicate his position of leadership in the home.
They are still courting.	They take each other for granted.
He has little parental responsibility.	He resents pressure to be more of a family man.
She accepts the role of a homemaker.	She begins to resent being tied to the home.
Empathetic in illness.	Intolerant of many physical problems.
She more readily accepts a submissive role.	She resents his authority.
Attempt to please each other.	Focus on pleasing self.
More communication on decisions and plans.	Tendency to act independently.

The list could go on and on. Yet it is sufficient to demonstrate that significant changes do take place over the years. The first step in correction is recognition of the need. Take a moment as a couple and put a check by each comparison in the list which applies to you in some way.

There are additional comparisons that shed light on marriage in mid-life. Husbands and wives frequently develop divergent value systems and priorities in mid-life. The wife generally wants the marriage to grow in depth. She cannot live with the status quo. The husband is complacent and satisfied as long as there is no open conflict and if the physical relationship is fairly good. The wife begins to focus more on security in both their relationship and in their financial arrangements. He tends to be risky as he views his last chance to change jobs or make it big. She wants more verbal appreciation, whereas he tends to be less appreciative and communicative. The wife wants more affection. He wants better sex. She wants more understanding, especially in physical and emotional issues. He also wants more understanding, but in job and career issues. The wife becomes fatalistic, thinking the relationship will never change. He doesn't even see that a change is needed.

Thus, without significant mutual consideration, discussion, and effort, conflict and misunderstandings ensue. Mary and I have seen many of these symptoms in our marriage and can now identify several vulnerable points. In several areas it is still difficult for us to see each other's viewpoint. But as we consider these issues, our deep love, and our commitment to each other and to our marriage, give us a base from which to work.

The Major Issues
We can identify certain major tendencies:

1. In mid-life there will be role changes and reversals especially in the areas of leadership, material needs, and spiritual matters.
2. The greatest failure in mid-life is the failure to realize that we have both changed and will keep changing.
3. A growing independence can lead to selfishness.
4. Failure to aggressively deepen and strengthen a marriage in the midst of differences and conflict will make it more vulnerable to divorce.

Communication

One evening our youngest daughter, Kris, was talking to

me. I was preoccupied and looking away. Suddenly she grabbed both my cheeks, turned my face to hers and continued her conversation at a three-inch, nose-to-nose distance. She didn't just want to talk. She wanted to be heard and to know she was being heard. This is the essence of communication.

Next to our basic biblical commitment to love, communication is the most important factor in marriage. It is even more crucial in mid-life for without good communication, the issues cannot be talked through and resolved. In the insecurities of mid-life we need to hear our partner say, "I love you," and, "I care about how you feel."

It would be presumptuous to try to condense all the pertinent principles of communication in this brief section.[1] Here we will simply summarize some of the issues and principles we believe are key to communication in mid-life.

Varying Levels and Intensity

No one is able to maintain deep and meaningful communication 100 percent of the time. We all engage in small talk, opinions, and many other kinds of conversation which do not reveal our deepest feelings.

Levels of communication have been defined in many ways. The most common level is a greeting, introductory question, or cliche conversation. (How was your day? How are you doing? It's a beautiful day.) This is how we test the water for further interaction. We need to know that the door is open for more significant conversation. Some of it is simply being polite and gracious.

Imagine the absurdity of a husband walking in from work, finding his wife in the kitchen frantically juggling a meatloaf in one hand, turning on the oven, telling the children to wait for help in fixing their hair, and giving her husband a perfunctory kiss. Then he says, "Darling, tell me how you really feel, deep down inside, about our marriage." What she needs is a quick kiss and a helping hand.

We then move to factual communication on events, children, job, and plans. (Kathy needs a ride to church tonight. I had a hectic day. You got a letter from your parents today. The car is running poorly.) There may be some additional emotional overtones and meanings, but we are mainly still communicating facts. Our reaction to the facts sets the stage for deeper communication.

Frequently we do not want to reveal ourselves and our own thinking in a conversation, so we discuss things in the third person. (John says there's a real problem brewing at church. I heard that the Biggs are having trouble selling their house. The boss really got upset at Ed's mistakes on that contract. The kids feel we are too strict on their hours and restrictions.) We find it easier to discuss other people's feelings, beliefs and faults than our own. It is important to discuss things in the third person, both for information and for a lead-in to more personalized conversation.

We next venture into the level of expressing our opinions. (I think the boss was unfair to Ed. I think we need to have a discussion with the kids on their relationship to each other. I believe we need new leadership in our city. I think Judy was wrong in her responses to Patty last week.) Here we reveal more of ourselves. We offer a mental opinion. Note that most of the statements make us vulnerable if someone disagrees. The security of our relationship determines how much of our thinking we will reveal.

Finally, we express our feelings. (The children really made me angry today. I feel like you don't really understand what I am saying. When we talk about finances, I feel guilty because I spend quite a bit on food.)

Feelings and facts are often unrelated. We do not always know why we feel as we do. But yet we desperately need to express these feelings to our partners without fear of rejection. Men especially need to learn to express more of their feelings and to accept their wife's expressions without rejection. Women need to understand that an honest expression of feelings comes harder for men. Women should not base their evaluation of their marriage on feelings alone.

Analyze yourself and each other. Correction in habits of communication cannot take place before a need is recognized. Therefore, it is crucial that you recognize the patterns of your own communication. Remember that your communication with your mate may differ considerably from your communication with others. You might be very sensitive and open to others and still clam up when communicating with your mate.

Recall the events of the last two weeks. Then answer the following questions:

1. How much time did we spend talking privately?
2. On how many days did we get at least fifteen minutes of private communication?
3. Did we discuss at least one issue on the "feeling" level without anger?
4. Did I initiate any conversations on the "feeling" level?
5. Was there any issue discussed in the last two weeks where I did not feel understood?

These questions will give you some idea as to how well you communicate with each other. Discuss your answers with your mate.

Communication takes time and effort. Few worthwhile accomplishments come easily or naturally. They require work. Communication is no different. We must study ourselves and our mates. We need humility in admitting some faults and needs. We must make a commitment to change and work on improving our communication.

Remember that habits developed over many years do not change easily or quickly. It will take time and effort. Is your commitment to good communication with your mate deep enough to take the time required? Without both a commitment and the necessary time, communication will never develop in your marriage.

Listen and understand. When communication takes place between two people, one of them must listen. Talking to someone who is obviously not hearing you, but who is pretending to listen, crushes your ego and can destroy the relationship.

How do you listen? Some listen to refute. Some listen to criticize. Some listen to be polite. Some listen to remember. And some listen to understand. How many times have you heard the complaint, "But he just doesn't hear me. He doesn't understand."? We all recall times when we desperately tried to be understood but felt like we were hitting our heads against a brick wall.

In mid-life we commonly see couples give up and resign themselves to never being understood by each other. They have reached what seems to be a permanent impasse. Yet the solution is often quite simple. If one of the partners would simply resolve to listen completely without rebuke or argument while trying to really understand, the breakthrough would come. We have found that especially in times of discouragement, the wife does not want discussion, just a listening, sympathetic ear. Are you willing to just listen?

But how can we go from simply listening to the deeper

level of understanding? There are two key issues—what was factually said, and what was intended. No one expresses his feelings and thoughts perfectly. Speech is an imperfect and inaccurate means of communication. One technique is to repeat in your own words what you thought you heard and ask if you understood correctly. Another helpful thing is to ask non-threatening questions. Threatening questions are, "Why do you say that?", "Are you sure that is true?", or, "Why did you do that?". Non-threatening and helpful questions could be, "Could you say that in another way to help me get the idea?", "Would you repeat that idea since I'm not sure I got it?", or, "Can you give me an illustration of what you mean?". Most "why" questions are threatening.

It is vital to pray for understanding and wisdom in relationships. During mid-life, good communication will encourage both husband and wife through times of stress and change. Without it you are alone in your struggle. We desperately need the companionship of intimate communication. There is no substitute.

Learn to resolve conflict. Resolving conflict is one of the most significant kinds of communication. Conflict prevents some forms of communication and initiates other kinds. Life and marriage are filled with conflict. Life doesn't remain at a high pitch of conflict, but conflict is always present in some form. As we mentioned earlier in the chapter, the frequency of conflict in mid-life is greater since we become more critical, less tolerant, and possibly more selfish. Thus conflicts are often sharper, deeper, and of a more lasting nature. Thus, resolution is imperative.[2]

We need to see some of these issues addressed by Scripture. Consider the principles in these passages:

- "Instead, speaking the truth in love, we will in

all things grow up into him who is the Head, that is, Christ" (Ephesians 4:15). Principle: Truth must be spoken in an attitude of love. Being truthful is part of our growth in Christ. This verse is in the context of teaching on the Body of Christ and applies in marriage.

- "Do not let any unwholesome talk come out of your mouths, but only what is helpful for building others up according to their needs that it may benefit those who listen" (Ephesians 4:29). Principle: Our speech is to be constructive rather than destructive.

- "Be kind and compassionate to one another, forgiving each other, just as in Christ God forgave you" (Ephesians 4:32). Principle: Kindness and forgiveness must be our attitudes in our communications with each other.

- "A gentle answer turns away wrath, but a harsh word stirs up anger. The tongue of the wise commends knowledge, but the mouth of the fool gushes folly" (Proverbs 15:1-2). Principle: If we communicate softly and gently we will avoid anger and conflict. Think of how many conflicts this advice could have prevented.

- "He who answers before listening—that is his folly and his shame" (Proverbs 18:13). Principle: We must listen completely before responding.

- "A word aptly spoken is like apples of gold in settings of silver" (Proverbs 25:11). Principle: Good communication is valuable beyond description. Not only the right words, but also the right timing counts toward positive relationships.

Many Scripture passages highlight the need for godly communications. Though certainly not unique to mid-life, the need for good communication in marriage is a must for building or rebuilding the proper foundations for the future.

The Sexual Relationship

Ron and Linda were forty, had three lovely children, good careers, responsible positions in the church, and an outwardly happy family. In a matter of months their marriage exploded and dissolved. A postmortem revealed two key issues.

The first was an almost complete absence of meaningful communication. He dominated and she submitted. The second was a completely unsatisfying sexual relationship. There was conflict over birth control and she feared becoming pregnant again. She was too cold and passive for him. But although these problems had existed for years, neither one ever sought help until it was too late.

Mid-life can be the beginning of an entirely new enjoyment and fulfillment in the physical area of marriage, or it can be the source of constant dissatisfaction and conflict. So many things occur emotionally and physically during this period that the sexual relationship is often neglected, largely because husbands and wives do not understand themselves or each other at this stage of life. We will highlight some of the key issues confronting a couple's physical relationship in mid-life.

Varying Sexual Drives

No human being remains the same emotionally or physically. We change hourly, daily, monthly, and yearly. One of the earliest lessons a young couple learns is the monthly physical and emotional cycle caused by the wife's menstrual period. Conflicts and misunderstandings are often due to a lack of consideration for this cycle.

But there is another variation which is crucial to the understanding of the sexual relationship in mid-life. Refer to the graph in Figure 7-1. This graph does not hold true for every person, but simply demonstrates average sexual drive for most people. A man reaches his sexual peak (in terms of innate physical drive) between eighteen and twenty-five. His drive then begins to diminish with age. However, barring specific physical illness, he can remain sexually active into his sixties and seventies, and beyond. A woman reaches her maximum sexual drive from thirty to forty. She is not necessarily more fertile, but her desire for sex and her personal enjoyment are greatest at this age.

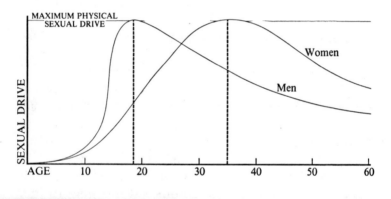

Figure 7-1

A man in his twenties responds primarily at the physical level and secondarily on the emotional level. As his physical drive decreases, these levels reverse. In his thirties and forties he becomes more dependent on his emotional drive.

The woman in her twenties is largely dependent on emotional stimulation for fulfillment in the sexual relationship. She then blooms sexually in her thirties as she develops greater physical desire. There are a number of reasons for this change in a woman.

In her early years the burden of childbearing and a fear of possible pregnancy often inhibits her from totally enjoying the physical relationship. Young wives often feel "used" as they desire more tender, emotional involvement and see an overriding physical drive in their husband. Also, some women do not become orgasmic till they have been married several years. When they do, their physical drive increases significantly.[3]

When a couple recognizes and understands these differences and changes they can more readily develop their relationship in mid-life. The way you build the sexual relationship in your thirties and early forties determines your long-term fulfillment in your fifties and sixties.

One other observation is in order. A woman's entire sexual development is eventually altered by the menopause or a hysterectomy (with ovaries also removed). Certainly this affects sexual drive due to the hormonal imbalance in the body. Some women go through menopause with little difficulty. Others suffer physical and emotional trauma. The sexual relationship need not suffer or change drastically either in ability or enjoyment. Several things can ease the change.

1. Both husband and wife should understand the physical process of menopause.
2. A woman with a positive mental attitude toward the change will fare much better. The one who ponders every negative aspect and who attributes her every physical and emotional problem to menopause will

have a great deal of difficulty.
3. Doctors regularly prescribe hormone replacements to offset the marked change in a woman's body.
4. An understanding and patient husband will be the greatest help in the menopausal transition.

Many women destroy their fulfillment of the sexual relationships by using the menopause as a reason for not responding to their husbands. Abstinence is not necessary and would be harmful to their total relationship. But adjusting to menopause requires the cooperation and consideration of both husband and wife.

Due to the emotional issues husbands face in mid-life, they may temporarily lose their sexual desire. Then a greater stimulus is needed for arousing sexual interest.

A Maturing Sexual Relationship

During mid-life the sexual relationship can and should be the most fulfilling of any time in marriage. But it will not happen automatically. You must plan for it and work toward it.

The key to a fulfilling sexual relationship in mid-life is the *desire to please one another*. Scripture instructs us to "rejoice in the wife of your youth" (Proverbs 5:18). Love for another person motivates us to serve and please them. God's command is, "Husbands, love your wives, just as Christ loved the church and gave himself up for her" (Ephesians 5:25). This kind of love seeks the best for the other. The husband serves his wife by loving her. The command to wives is, "Wives, submit to your husbands as to the Lord" (Ephesians 5:22). But why should wives submit to the Lord? Because they love the Lord and wish to serve him. True submission is not the result of fear, but of love and a desire to please or serve.

The next key is *understanding each other's drives and needs*. Study your mate. Know what he or she is going through. Even better, anticipate what they will go through and prepare for it. Talk over their needs and problems. Some husbands need to learn what their wife is going through. Some wives need to discover what their husband is experiencing emotionally which also affects him sexually. The better we understand each other, the more we develop in our relationship.

Be willing to discuss the issues. Many couples do not discuss their sexual relationship except during a conflict or when complaining. When changes occur, communication can bridge the gap of understanding. Be willing to learn. Consider reading and discussing together the two books suggested in the footnotes.

A maturing sexual relationship is built upon mutual trust. In mid-life a man or woman must fully understand that the sexual relationship is only part of their total relationship. As you change, your sexual relationship will develop and change also. Growth in the sexual relationship is a process which takes time and effort. But many expect instant results instead of exercising patience and accepting gradual responses to changing needs.

When changes or problems develop, trust is the ingredient that produces growth rather than decay. When we know our partner is seeking our best, we can respond with trust. Many men and women react suspiciously in the midst of sexual conflicts, silently accusing their mates of manipulating them or faking a problem. Trust does not stoop to such thoughts. Trust seeks to help, not to accuse. Trust, coupled with sincere love, patiently builds; it does not tear down.

Yet even as the relationship matures, certain common problems frequently appear. The root problem in any sexual relationship is *selfishness*. Each partner wants to be totally satisfied and fulfilled. This view is the opposite of the desire to please one another. The selfish sexual relationship will never reach fulfilling maturity and will always be fraught with conflict.

A major complaint from women is the *fear of being used*, rather than loved. Especially in mid-life, when much reevaluation is occurring, a woman resents the idea of being an object of lust rather than a loved person. Then a woman must trust, and a man must learn unselfishness.

But the man in mid-life also harbors a fear. He is afraid he will not be able to perform sexually. In mid-life without the intense physical drive of his youth, he is more dependent on emotional stimulation. He is afraid of impotency. Aside from actual physical illness, such an occurrence is usually temporary and emotionally based. He tends to become embarrassed that he is now dependent on his wife's responses for his own. Thus his ego is hurt. This is one of the Lord's ways of making a man more sensitive and understanding of his wife's longstanding need for greater emotional involvement in their physical relationship. But, it can also give way to lust and cause him to seek fulfillment outside marriage.

The Problem of Lust in the Mid-life Marriage

Infidelity can occur at any time and for many reasons. Mid-life often presents a more fertile ground for lust to result in infidelity. Infidelity is a product of what the mind has harbored for months or years.

First, we will consider some of the specific reasons why lust develops and then some of its more basic roots. None of these factors should lead to infidelity when the marriage is properly founded on commitment to Christ and deep love for one another.

The man in mid-life sees himself growing older. Perhaps he is balding, and becoming pudgy. Even though he may be a tiger on the job, he may still battle a weak self-image. His wife and family bring additional pressures and demands. If another woman gives him attention, he feels flattered. His ego receives a boost. As he allows his mind and emotions to focus on a woman other than his wife, he begins to look outside marriage for personal enjoyment. There he finds only false enjoyment laced with poison and bitterness, but many men give in to its lures.

Women face a similar dilemma. In mid-life they desire deeper communication, so if they find a man who will listen, they begin to value this relationship, innocent though it may be, and to resent their husband.

If a woman works outside the home, she has many contacts with married, divorced, and single men who relate to her as a woman, often with the hope of developing an intimate relationship. They are usually polite, attentive, and receptive listeners. The contact can develop subtly with no intention of becoming more than a friendship and a release for tension. Soon she discovers her affections focusing on another man instead of her husband.

Another disparity develops when a husband becomes careless in his personal appearance, and even overweight, while his wife keeps trim and takes care of her personal appearance. The opposite can also happen. In either case, resentment and disapproval can build up until one of them begins seeking and receiving approval outside the marriage.

We often describe adultery or fornication as "falling into sin." But no one ever falls into that sin. That moment of indiscretion and immorality did not begin with the act. The seed was planted months or years before, first in the mind, then in various pre-sexual experiences, and finally there was the full act. The seed was watered and nurtured with repeated mental indiscretions and pre-sexual indulgences. The immoral incident simply picks the fruit which has grown in the mind.

"For from within, out of men's hearts, come evil thoughts, sexual immorality, theft, murder, adultery" (Mark 7:21). The process which leads to this kind of sin is described in James 1:15. "Then after desire has conceived, it gives birth to sin; and sin, when it is full grown gives birth to death."

The roots of sexual sin begin with a battle for sexual purity in the mind. What we think of constantly, we ultimately do. The importance of the mind is reflected in two biblical words.

The first is the Greek word *aselgeia* which is sometimes translated as sensuality. It is used in several passages. "The acts of the sinful nature are obvious: sexual immorality, impurity and debauchery [*aselgeia*]" (Galatians 5:19).

"So I tell you this and must insist on it in the Lord, that you must no longer live as the Gentiles do . . . Having lost all sensitivity they have given themselves over to *sensuality*, [*aselgeia*] so as to indulge in every kind of impurity, with a continual lust for more" (Ephesians 4:17, 19). Other translations render the word as *lasciviousness, licentiousness, debauchery,* and *lewdness.*

The dictionary defines sensual as "relating to or consisting in the gratification of the senses or the indulgence of appetite: fleshy, devoted to or preoccupied with the senses or appetites."[4]

The second word is the Greek word *epithumia* which is translated *lusts, passions, desires* or *cravings*. "Flee the evil desires [*epithumia*] of youth, and pursue righteousness" (2 Timothy 2:22). "Abstain from sinful desires [epithumia] which war against your soul'' (1 Peter 2:11). "For everything in the world—the cravings [*epithumia*] of sinful man, the lust [*epithumia*] of his eyes and the boasting of what he has and does comes not from the Father but from the world'' (1 John 2:16).

Since the mind is so significantly involved in sowing the seeds of sin, it must be guarded carefully. The sensory gates to the mind are the eyes, ears, and physical touch. Any of these senses can ignite sensual, lustful thoughts. Here we are not speaking of the sexual drive which is a gift from God, but of the sinful focusing of that drive outside marriage.

Television, billboards, and magazines bombard the mind with thoughts and ideas which lead to action. The external battle to influence and control the mind rages daily. The outcome of the battle, the only real control of the mind is left with the individual. We *choose* what we look at, read, or listen to. We cannot afford to sample and taste pornography on television or in print. Once it enters our mind it engraves its images in our brain. These thoughts may then germinate and lead to infidelity. Even when they do not lead to immorality in the body, they corrupt the mind and seriously influence the marital relationship. Protect your eyes and ears from inputs which arouse sensual and lustful thoughts toward anyone other than your mate.

One young woman was having real difficulties in her relationship with her husband. He simply did not measure up to her expectations. She was hooked on the television soap operas. There she saw virile heroes, extra-marital relationships, and divorce. She compared her husband to the actors, and found that he lacked their attractiveness and personality. She felt she was missing something and blamed him. Until she stopped watching these shows, their marriage was shaky.

Often when one has dutifully guarded the eyes and ears, another gate to the mind is left open—the touch. Friendly, supportive gestures and pats of encouragement demonstrate our affection and concern for one another. But when touches become too frequent or prolonged, we give or receive the wrong impression. When the physical presence or touch of another invites impure thoughts and desires, we need to evaluate that relationship. We should be kind and helpful to one another, exercising common courtesy, but we must also guard against crossing over the borderline into sensuality.

Several Scriptures counsel us regarding our minds. Hebrews 4:12-13 tells us that God's word "judges the thoughts and attitudes of the heart." In 2 Corinthians 10:5 Paul wrote, "We take captive every thought to make it obedient to Christ." Controlling the mind is a continual process. Do not conform any longer to the pattern of this world, but be transformed by the *renewing of your mind*. Then you will be able to test and approve what God's will is—his good, pleasing and perfect will" (Romans 12:2).

We are dealing with the central issue of preserving the wholeness of marriage. Grave spiritual danger lies in allowing sexual looseness to invade our minds and bodies. "Can a man scoop fire into his lap without his clothes being burned? Can a man walk on hot coals without his feet being scorched? So is he who sleeps with another man's wife" (Proverbs 6.27-29). Never allow the beauty of the sexual relationship in marriage to be tarnished by a sensual or lustful lifestyle.

But what does one do when lustful thoughts or conflicts spring up? We must recognize their reality and treat them specifically.

When such problems occur, the husband frequently responds by purchasing a sex manual, and reading it to see what his wife needs to do. He then gives it to her to read and heed. What does this communicate? His action says, "I am not satisfied with you. The fault is yours, so read up on what a wife should be like. Let me know when you have learned your lesson."

But sexual problems in marriage are not solely physical. They are symptoms of deeper problems. Here are some suggestions on how to deal with lust:

1. Recommit yourselves to each other verbally.
2. Examine your practice of holiness and purity of thought. If necessary, confess your need to God and recommit your mind to him.
3. Keep away from situations and inputs which provoke lustful thoughts.
4. Rebuild communication with your mate. Develop and practice patience as both of you go through emotional changes.
5. If lust is a part of your problem, prayerfully consider discussing it with your mate. This involves some risk since it reveals desire toward another. Yet it may awaken both of you to a need in your marriage and mobilize you to work together.
6. Memorize 1 Corinthians 10:13.
7. Review *together* your physical relationship. You may need to rebuild this part of your marriage on a right foundation of love and respect. Refer to the previously mentioned books by the LaHayes and the Wheats.

The Poison of Jealousy

"For where you have envy and selfish ambition, there you find disorder and every evil practice" (James 3:16). Jealousy poisons marriage. When you begin suspecting your mate of infidelity, or any level of a romantic relationship with another, you sow seeds of jealousy which destroy trust. Trust accompanied by love keeps a couple together.

Jack and Karen Johnson are in the latter part of mid-life. Over the years one characteristic of their marriage has overpowered all others. Karen is intensely jealous, conjuring up imaginative relationships which she is convinced Jack has had. Every unexplained absence is suspect. When he isn't available by phone, she considers it another proof. He is angered by her perpetual suspicion. Years of tension have taken their toll, and his disgust shows outwardly. Sadly, both are Christians. Their history reveals problems of infidelity by both of them in the first years of marriage. Now the memory of that and the accompanying guilt and pain keep cropping up and causing renewed distrust and jealousy. Her jealousy developed into hate and resentment followed by years of misery. No amount of logic or reason can persuade Karen that Jack has changed. She resents his outward innocence and slams his religious facade.

Jealousy stems from both imagination and fact. Generally, it is best to let your spouse know when you are jealous. But do not bring it up in an accusatory manner. No matter how you do it, there will be some conflict and strong discussion. There may even be hurt. But it is better to hurt a little now than a lot later. Be sure to admit that you may be wrong, but that you simply want to express what you feel inside.

Be prepared for one of three responses. The first is an absolute denial and reassurance of love and faithfulness. The second is admission of guilt substantiating your jealousy. The third response includes neither denial or admission, but involves an angry attack. In any of these cases, respond by accepting what is said. You may need to discuss it further to try to discover and eliminate the causes of jealousy. Some men and women are naturally friendly, and even flirtatious in action, without intending to hurt their mate. There may be unwise and careless behavior which needs to be corrected.

When actual infidelity has marred your relationship in the past, the danger of jealousy looms even larger. Your only protection is to commit your marriage totally to God and to trust both God and your mate. Ask yourself the question, "Have I truly forgiven him (or her) for that offense?" An unforgiving heart corrupts all future relationships. Or, if you were the guilty one, ask, "Did I ask forgiveness and did I repent of the sin before God and my mate?" You cannot change history, but you can keep from repeating it—but not if jealousy pervades your marriage relationship.

If such a discussion is unproductive, you may need to get counsel. But if you do, be careful not to do so with the view that you have all the evidence and your jealousy is justified. Many get counsel simply to publicly accuse their mate and gain sympathy. The purpose of counsel is to help solve the problem. Often an objective counselor can discern where we allowed imagination to run wild.

The jealous feeling may be so deep that no amount of reasoning or counsel can erase it. In that case you must realize that you will live with jealousy eating you up with no chance of respite. It is now a spiritual and psychological issue. Until God breaks down the barrier in your heart on this issue, no relief will come.

1 Corinthians 13:4-7 spells out the antidote to jealousy.

> Love is patient, love is kind. It does not envy, it does not boast, it is not proud. It is not rude, it is not self-seeking, it is not easily angered, it keeps no record of wrongs. Love does not delight in evil but rejoices

with the truth. It always protects, always trusts, always hopes, always perseveres.

Solomon gave the wisest counsel in the matter of keeping the sanctity of the marriage relationship.

> May your fountain be blessed, and may you rejoice in the wife of your youth. A loving doe, a graceful deer—may her breasts satisfy you always, may you ever be captivated by her love. Why be captivated, my son, by an adulteress? Why embrace the bosom of another man's wife? (Proverbs 5:18-20).

> For the lips of an adulteress drip honey, and her speech is smoother than oil; but in the end she is bitter as gall, sharp as a double-edged sword. Her feet go down to death; her steps lead straight to the grave. She gives no thought to the way of life; her paths are crooked, but she knows it not. Now then, my sons, listen to me; do not turn aside from what I say. Keep to a path far from her, do not go near the door of her house, lest you give your best strength to others and your years to one who is cruel'' (Proverbs 5:3-9).

Developing Your Marriage

We believe that mid-life is the best of all times in marriage. The frivolity of youth is replaced by the maturity of experience. The security of an intimate and trusting relationship gives freedom. The deepening of an already mature relationship yields satisfaction unlike any other achievement. The roots of a solid marriage give the stability necessary to face the demands of mid-life. Few couples wish to return to the frustration and anxious pressure of their first years of marriage. The excitement of the present overwhelms the vague past.

Even a good relationship must be protected and nurtured with great care. Here are some ways to protect and nurture your marriage in mid-life:

1. Accept your partner's limitations and faults just as God does—just as you want yours to be accepted.
2. Make a commitment to each other to have at least five minutes of communication daily. This is to be a private time without children or the television.
3. Take some time away together. We have found that two days is a bare minimum. You need not go far, or to an expensive place. Just go somewhere so that you can talk, read, be together, pray together, and develop your relationship. If you have not done this before, you may need to do it once or twice to learn how to relate without the normal flurry of activity.
4. Make a commitment to God and to each other to grow in your marriage. Many have found marriage enrichment seminars very helpful. Most churches can direct you to such developmental activities.
5. Help and encourage each other to grow and develop. Help your spouse to reach his or her goals. This necessitates knowing your spouse's needs, aspirations, and goals.
6. Recommit yourself to spiritual growth. Your marriage will not improve if you do not grow in your intimacy with God. All the psychological tools and seminars will be of little value if your individual relationship with God is not developing.
7. Guard against bitterness and jealousy. These poisons will undermine growth.

Don't miss the greatest opportunity of your married life to develop and deepen your marriage. Neglect and abandonment of your marriage in mid-life leaves a void in your life which can never be filled. But careful nurture and renewed commitments to one another and to God will make your marriage the most satisfying of all human relationships, for it will still stand when career and material achievements fade like smoke from a dying fire. Guard your marriage. Nurture it. Develop it. Enjoy each other!

NOTES: 1. Two good books are *Getting to know You,* by Marjorie Umphrey (Irvine, California: Harvest House Publishers, 1976), and *Family Communication,* by Sven Wahlroos (New York: Macmillan Publishing Co., 1974).

2. David Augsburger, *Caring Enough to Confront* (Glendale, California: Gospel Light/Regal Books, 1973).

3. Ed and Gaye Wheat, *Intended for Pleasure* (Old Tappan, New Jersey: Fleming H. Revell Co., 1977).

4. *Webster's New Colllegiate Dictionary,* (Springfield, Massachusetts: G. & C. Merriam Company, 1973), page 1056.

CHAPTER 8

Children

Teenagers

John sat propped against the headboard of his bed staring into the darkness, his mind churning. His wife, Carol, slept quietly beside him. For weeks he had struggled with frustration at work. He had been employed by one manufacturing company since he graduated from college. His supervisor obviously appreciated his work, and John knew he was a valued employee. But twice in recent weeks younger men were promoted ahead of him. He realized that while he thought he was still climbing for the top, he had, in fact, already arrived at his personal summit.

His mind raced. Shall I look for a job in another company? What if I stay and they decide to fire me? No, they couldn't. I've been with them almost twenty-five years. But, what if they do anyway? How would we manage? The twins start college next year. We'd never make it.

The shrill sound of the telephone shattered the stillness. John grabbed the receiver.

"Hello."

"John, that you? This is Harry Bergman."

"Sure, Harry. Is there anything wrong? It's kind of late."

"Yeah, I know it's late, but I had to call. We've got trouble, John."

"Trouble? What do you mean?"

"Well, you know your George and my Debbie have been dating lately. Well, they're over here now and they say they're going to get married before they graduate from high school. How's that for a kick in the head?"

"Married!" John shouted. "Those crazy kids!"

Carol stirred. "What is it? What's wrong?" she asked. She sat up and switched on the lamp.

John turned to her. "George and Debbie told Harry they're going to get married before they finish high school. Can you believe it? They're just kids, for Pete's sake!"

He turned back to the phone, "Harry, keep those kids right there. Carol and I are coming over." He slammed the phone down.

"As if I didn't already have enough on my mind," he fumed. "What can George be thinking of? Why can't he be more like his brother? Matt never gives us any trouble."

"John, calm down," urged Carol. "We can't go over to Harry's feeling upset and angry. Let's simmer down, pray, and then go talk to them."

"You're right, Carol. It's just that I'm so worried about my job—and now this. I'm sorry."

John and Carol experienced one of the most common, yet perplexing aspects of raising teens. The rebellion, frustrations, and struggles of teenagers impact heavily on us because so often they coincide with our mid-life transitions.

We love our teens and assume they love us too, but our darling toddlers have disappeared. In their places stand defiant, struggling teenagers demanding freedom from the restraints and counsel which we insist are necessary for their health, well-being, and future. If only they realized how wise we are and what lessons our years have taught us! We could help them avoid so many disastrous situations and decisions. We wish they would just arrange to have their crises at times when we are free from emotional pressures.

But life doesn't accommodate us conveniently. We need to be spiritually and emotionally prepared and willing to invest all of our physical and emotional resources in helping our children to maturity.

While parents of young children may express dread as they anticipate the teen years, the struggles teens go through can be minor compared to the joys they can bring their parents.

Too often parents feel that as children grow they require proportionately less time. So parents increase their pace and fill their schedules accordingly. That is not a good plan. Teens demand less of our time, but want our attention on *their* terms. They maintain busy schedules and expect our time and attention when *they* request, want, or need it. If we refuse to be available to them when they are free, if we are too tired to talk when they come in at night, if we allow the pressures of our interests and commitments to crowd them aside, they will soon stop sharing. Then we will really lose them.

We reveal ourselves to our children in our responses. We are more transparent than we like to think. They easily detect our true responses to them.

Problem Responses to Teenagers

Anger. Most anger arises as a result of a personal offense or infringement on someone's rights. If in our mid-years we haven't developed a tolerance for the thoughtless infringements of our rights by others, we will remain perpetually angry with our teenagers.

Only the most mature and sensitive teens will sympathetically recognize their parents' struggles and respond appropriately. They simply do not have the life experience to appreciate the pressures we experience and the needs we feel. Most teens assume that people in mid-life, their parents included, have put life all together and have no appreciation or understanding of the crucial issues they are facing.

If we bristle every time our teenagers rebel or act inappropriately, we will convey an attitude of hostility and anger towards them. Patience provides the answer to anger with teens. The apostle Paul understood this principle when he explained to Timothy that we should "correct, rebuke and encourage—with great patience and careful instruction" (2 Timothy 4:2). Controlling our anger will reduce conflict with our teens. Proverbs reinforces this thought. "A hot tempered man stirs up dissension, but a patient man calms a quarrel" (Proverbs 15:18). Proverbs 15:1 adds, "A gentle answer turns away wrath, but a harsh word stirs up anger."

Resentment. Perhaps we don't chafe with anger against our teenagers, but we do feel resentment against them for their problems, music, friends, poor grades, sloppiness, indifference to family members, and their emotional outbursts.

One mother said of her seventeen-year-old son, "I'm his cook and laundress. He doesn't appreciate anything I do for him. He never says thanks. In fact, he hardly speaks to me and I resent him for it. It will be a happy day around here when he moves out." Although she didn't say that in her son's hearing, no doubt he had already sensed his mother's attitude and withered under her animosity.

Teenagers need all of the support we can provide. When they sense resentment, they will cover their hurt with a tough "I-don't-care" exterior. Teens desperately want the commendation and approval of their parents. Resentment, covert or open, may erase any supportive statement. We need to recognize resentment as a sin against one of God's people, confess it, and resolve to love and appreciate our child for his potential. We should minimize criticism, and increase genuine praise.

Worry. Webster's New Collegiate Dictionary defines worry as "mental distress or agitation resulting from concern, usually for something impending or anticipated."[1] Worry increases proportionately as our control of our teenagers decreases. We may recognize and accept the wisdom of letting go, but the possibilities overwhelm us. Teenagers can so easily make wrong choices. Their judgment seems limited and undeveloped. They have made mistakes before and we feel sure they will make mistakes again. Unscrupulous people might take advantage of them. Maybe they'll reject the spiritual teaching we've given them. Or suppose they experiment with drugs, or become sexually promiscuous?

For years we have guided their actions and watched them respond. We are unprepared for their surge toward independence. We know it must come. We have dedicated our parenting to guiding them toward mature and responsible adulthood, but when they break those bonds, we feel anxious.

How quickly our minds turn to anxiety and worry rather than to prayer. Paul recorded the Lord's beautiful and practical answer to worry in Philippians 4:6-7: "Do not be anxious about anything, but in everything, by prayer and petition, with thanksgiving, present your requests to God. And the peace of God, which transcends all understanding, will guard your hearts and your minds in Christ Jesus." We must commit our teens to God.

Failure. Solomon wrote in Proverbs 10:1, "A wise son brings joy to his father, but a foolish son grief to his mother." Perhaps Solomon penned those words with a sense of failure and disappointment over his own children.

As our children pass through their teens, we desperately want them to become faithful disciples of Jesus Christ and productive citizens. If they veer from our expectations, we are filled with a sense of failure.

Perhaps they choose a lifestyle we disapprove. Maybe they won't fulfill our expectations in a career field. We may experience embarrassment and shame when others ask about our children. The insensitive questions and comments of family and friends only increase our frustration and disappointment.

But we must ask ourselves if we want them to be like us, or do we want them to be like Jesus Christ? Can we trust God to work in them and for them? Can we accept them, and ourselves, as they struggle through their difficult periods?

We must believe that God will work in their lives. We are responsible to pray for them, to influence as much as we can, while continuing to love and accept them.

Pressure. We feel keenly the need for maximizing the teen years with our children. Pressure comes from:

- the brevity of time remaining with them
- their problems during our mid-life transitions
- their unpredictable behavior
- their emotional upheavals
- the friends they select
- their hectic schedules
- the life choices they make

If you have more than one teen in your home, you may feel that you are fighting fires on several fronts at once. As a crisis in one child's life ends, a different problem flares up in the life of another. Pressure remains a reality throughout life.

Pressures from our children and their needs should drive us to a deeper dependence on God. He may not change the situation, but our confidence in his sovereignty will lift the pressure we feel. David understood this principle when he wrote in Psalm 37:28, 39: "For the Lord loves the just and will not forsake his faithful ones. . . .The salvation of the righteous comes from the Lord; he is their stronghold in time of trouble."

Projecting Our Values

When we reach our mid-years, we have developed a fairly firm value system. We know what receives attention in our lives. We emphasize and spend time in certain activities but not others. We value highly some attitudes, activities, accomplishments, and relationships.

What value system do you project to your teens? Do you want them to pattern themselves after you? Could you, like the Apostle Paul, say, "Even though you have ten thousand guardians in Christ, you do not have many fathers, for in Christ Jesus I became your father through the gospel. Therefore I urge you to imitate me" (1 Corinthians 4:15-16).

Or do we tell our children, "Don't do as I do. Do as I say"? Is there a disparity between the counsel we give our children and the way we live? What values should teens observe in their parents' lives?

Spiritual discipline. Our teenagers should be firmly convinced from personal observation that we believe and apply the word of God, that we spend time praying, and that we reach out to others. We need to let them see us fellowshipping with other Christians, and contributing in some way to the Body of Christ. They also need to know of our concern for those who don't know Christ. They should be aware that we give to missions. We should include them in many aspects of our spiritual life. How many parents ask their children to pray for them regularly, for instance?

We cannot depend on the church alone to fully communicate spiritual values to our teenagers. Our example speaks far more loudly and shapes their attitudes toward God directly. We can give our children no greater heritage than knowing that we love God and are committed to practicing a life of discipleship.

Teenagers demonstrate great perception and can easily detect hypocrisy. One eighteen-year-old boy said, "You wouldn't believe my dad. He's on the church board and teaches Sunday school and everybody thinks he's a big deal, but at home he yells at Mom and thinks I'm nothing. Everybody else seems to think he's a great Christian, but I know better. I've never seen or heard him read the Bible at home—unless he is getting ready to be a super Christian in front of his Sunday school class."

The Israelites were encouraged to express spiritual values to their children in Deuteronomy 6:4-7.

> Hear, O Israel: the Lord our God, the Lord is one. Love the Lord your God with all your heart and with all your soul and with all your strength. These commandments that I give you today are to be upon your hearts. Impress them on your children. Talk about them when you sit at home and when you walk along the road, when you lie down and when you get up.

What spiritual values will your children learn from you?

Career

Bill determined as a young man that he would rise to the top of his company. His two sons grew up rarely seeing him during the week. He caught a train for the city before they woke up and often worked late into the evening at his office. When his sons were in high school, his long-suffering wife persuaded him to attend a weekend conference emphasizing responsible parenting.

When he learned the biblical approach to effectively communicating with and leading teens to a productive spiritual adulthood, Bill was appalled at the meager investment he had made in the lives of his children. He remembered how often his wife had encouraged him to participate in activities with his sons, and to work less, and spend more time at home. But he felt she responded too negatively to his career. After all, didn't he provide everything the boys could possibly want? They each owned a car, took ski lessons in the winter, and attended the best camps in the summer.

When the Holy Spirit convicted Bill of his neglect, he determined to reverse his misguided patterns. But to his chagrin, his sons rejected his attempts.

"Hey, Dad," his oldest son said. "We're all set, you know? I guess you mean well, but we're pretty busy now. Maybe when we were little we could have done some activities together, but not now."

Bill felt the rebuff keenly, but didn't let it deter him from his attempt to salvage a relationship with his children. He stopped staying late at the office and began arriving home every night for dinner. He was amazed his job didn't suffer. Only occasionally did he bring any work home. He found, though, that his sons were often absent because of their commitments. Bill spent hours praying alone and with his wife for their children. Gradually, after months of consistent time at home, Bill's sons realized he was sincere. He noticed they stayed home more often in the evenings and would clear a Saturday morning to go fishing with him.

Bill regreted his wasted years, but knew he had to live in the present. He was firmly convinced he should spend as much time as possible with his sons before they left home.

Our teenagers know when they are shunted aside and a career is given priority in the parent's life. Parents don't need to verbalize their priorities. Teens can read the signs only too well.

God will hold us accountable for the dedication and effort we invest in rearing our children. Career advancement will never compenslate for resentful, rebellious children.

Time

Do you really believe James 4:14? James wrote, "Why, you do not even know what will happen tomorrow. What is your life? You are a mist that appears for a little while and then vanishes."

If you were firmly convinced your life was as fragile and momentary as a breath on a frosty morning, would you change any of your involvements and activities? Would your teenager notice any difference in your schedule?

How often we choose insignificant or unproductive activities to crowd our precious hours. We subconsciously believe we are immune to the waste of irreplaceable time. Do our teens see us giving time to people, or do they see us pursuing personal pleasures? If we had to choose between time with them and personal activities, what would we do? Would we choose an evening of television instead of personal, undisturbed time with them? What priority do they receive in our schedules? Our children should be aware that they can interrupt our schedules at any time and know that we will do our utmost to accommodate them.

Obviously, some occasions will arise when our activites must exclude our children, but they should be infrequent and carefully explained.

For several years, as the travel commitments in our work and ministry have increased, we have felt more pressure between our family involvement and work. We have learned to place our chldren's activities on our schedules *first*, then we plan our travel and ministry around them as much as possible. We record the dates of their sports competitions, musical performances, and church activities. If we must be absent, we make a phone call immediately following the event to let the child give a fresh account of the experience and to reassure them of our interest and support.

Our daughter was competing in a sports event. Because of out-of-town commitments, we could not be there. "You won't be there! Who will I perform for then?" she asked. Her participation was bolstered by our attendance, so if we were absent she felt that keenly. We arranged to have a favorite aunt watch the event, and that reassured her of the family's interest and support.

We are amazed and disheartened when we attend many school activities where only a very few parents are present. We realize parents cannot attend everything. We have observed that parental attendance dwindles as the child's age increases. Nursery school functions are well attended by proud parents, but high school activities are poorly attended. During the teen years it is doubly important to show a personal interest in the activities of our children.

Teenagers need the reassurance of observing their

parents committing their time to lasting values—spiritual endeavors and people's lives.

Whenever we attempt to communicate values as parents, (and it happens whether or not we consciously strive to impart a value system) we must present a united front. One mother told us, "My husband doesn't like the family to watch much television. He wants the children to read instead. But when he's not around, we do our own thing."

Such a pattern communicates that:

- Dad's opinion is not respected.
- Mom sides with the children against Dad.
- entertainment is preferable to personal discovery.
- disagreements can be resolved by deception.

In Ephesians 6:1 the Scripture teaches, "Children, obey your parents in the Lord, for this is right." The agreement of both parents is implied. No one can obey contradictory commands. In order to foster respect and influence our teenagers properly, we must practice a harmonious pattern of parenting. Parents need to discuss the issues privately and agree on a decision. Even when one parent does not fully agree, full support is needed unless the decision is dangerous or very clearly incorrect.

The Death of One's Child in Mid-life

Many mid-life events come and go, but a son or daughter cannot be replaced. The death of a son or daughter in the mid-life years, especially the death of a teen or young adult, sends the mid-life parent through one of the deepest problems of life.

Roy and Glenda McFarlin, friends of ours, lost their twenty-year-old daughter, Terri Sue, in a sudden accident.

Glenda shared the impact this event had in their lives:

"Our first reaction was simply shock. It was three weeks before we asked the question, 'Why?' After the initial shock, we became angry, six days later, not so much at God, but at our daughter. We felt angry because she had allowed this to happen to her and because of the way we were suffering. Our anger was irrational, but very real.

"Then we entered a period of guilt. Guilt over our anger, guilt because we were questioning God, and guilt for the things we had not done for Terri Sue.

"Then one night I woke up thinking, 'I don't want to live.' To my own surprise, I was contemplating suicide. I called a friend who recognized the symptoms and immediately began praying for me on the phone. In a few moments the desire to end my life left, but I was shocked it even occurred.

"Our sense of loss was unbearable. Since Terri Sue was an only child, we knew we would never have a wedding, a baby shower, or a grandchild. We were too old to adopt or have another child. She left a void that would never be filled. It is not the same as losing a parent. They have usually lived a full life. But the death of a child is totally different.

"We are still trying to cope with our loss. But God has helped us. For the first time in our lives, we understand the significance of God sending his only Son to die. We also felt the anguish Mary must have experienced when Jesus was crucified. The constant encouragement and presence of our friends and pastor helped us significantly. For the first three weeks we were rarely alone. People were always there to bear the burden with us. Life will never be the same for us, but we know God will sustain and provide."

We have seen others go through a similar loss. Our cousin, Ron Nelson, was killed in a tragic truck accident in his early twenties. He was a vibrant, gracious, young man who any parent would be proud to claim. His sensitive concern for a younger invalid brother reflected his personal faith in Christ. He lived sacrificially. The impact of Ron's death on his parents, Willard and Arlene Nelson, cannot be described.

The death of a child of any age is difficult, but parents who lose a child during their child's teen years or twenties seem to recover more slowly and respond differently. As we enter mid-life, such an event overshadows all others. Somehow it alters the very course of life from then on. At that point God can enter our lives to comfort us and meet our needs. Our only other choice is to become bitter and angry at God and never allow him to sustain and help.

Another man, whose son was killed at age sixteen, said, "I turned to heaven and shook my fist at God. I swore at him. I hated God and cursed him. But it was my loss. I had no comfort. It took a couple of years to reconcile myself to the loss and to God. I wish I had turned to God sooner."

King David was in mid-life when his son, Absalom, died in battle. No one could soothe his grief. He wept, "O my son Absalom! My son, my son Absalom! If only I had died instead of you—O Absalom, my son, my son!" (2 Samuel 18:33). Grief over a death is largely grief over the void in our own lives. Should the memory be erased? No, for then deep lessons from God would be lost. Should there be no grief? No, for then we would not be human. Should our grief last forever? No, for then we would not allow God to comfort and encourage us. Should this experience draw us to God? Yes, for only in him can such a loss be understood and accepted. We must understand that his purposes go beyond this life to eternity where true life goes on. God never makes a mistake as to his timing for any life. Paul reflected on death in Philippians 1:21-23:

> For to me, to live is Christ and to die is gain. If I am to go on living in the body, this will mean fruitful labor for me. Yet what shall I choose? I do not know! I am torn between the two: I desire to depart and be with Christ, which is better by far.

Unfortunately, some young people die without ever receiving Christ. This emphasizes our need to lead our children to Christ as soon as possible. Remember, God is sufficient to meet our every need, even one so deep as the loss of a child, if we will but allow him to minister to us on a day-by-day basis.

Maturing Relationships

Spiritual Interaction. While our teens are still our physical children, after receiving Christ they become our brothers and sisters in Christ also. One of the great joys of parenting Christian teens comes when we fellowship with them on a spiritual level. No other communication cements our love as does spiritual interaction. As our teens mature and grow in Christ, we experience some of the most rewarding and satisfying moments of mid-life.

The Apostle John understood this and wrote, "It has given me great joy to find some of your children walking in the truth, just as the Father commanded us" (2 John 4).

We need to be willing to learn from our children. If they mention a bad attitude we have shown, or an unkind remark we have spoken, we need to thank them for their observation, ask their forgiveness, and resolve to change. Too often we respond defensively. When we receive their suggestions we enrich our own lives and our relationship with them. This will not undermine our authority; it will demonstrate our humility and teachability—qualities we want to see reproduced in their lives.

We should foster an atmosphere where teenagers can freely express their spiritual concerns and receive understanding and encouragement. Do you converse freely about God in your home? Can your teens freely share their successes and failures with you without fear of censure?

How would you respond to these comments?

"I talked to my friend at school today and asked her if she would like to hear what the Bible teaches about being a Christian. She said, 'No.' Period. Boy, did I feel stupid."

"I tried to have a quiet time today, but I just didn't feel like it, so I didn't. And my day was lousy."

"I don't think our family prays enough together. How come we don't pray more? Dad, are you going to do anything about that?"

Spiritual interaction on issues like these draws us closer to our teenagers and allows us to influence them. Allow the joys of fellowship with your teenagers to enrich your life.

Communication. Dr. Joe Aldrich, the president of Multnomah School of the Bible, has said, "As our children mature, we should move from a point of correction to a point of counsel."

At least eighteen times in the first eight chapters of Proverbs Solomon specifically addresses his son (or his children) and gives them counsel. (See Proverbs 1:8, 3:1, 3:11-12, 4:1, 5:1, and 7:1 for examples.)

By the time our children reach their teens we can no longer control them with correction and punishment. We may try, but it seldom works. Gentle counsel that guides them toward proper decisions is far more effective.

Many parents desperately try to control their teenagers by intimidation. When a conflict arises, they crush the child with sarcasm, ridicule, overwhelming logic, or anger. Although they hate themselves later, many parents seem powerless to make the shift from controlling toddlers to counseling teens. The adolescent may comply with his parent's orders, but inwardly he seethes with resentment and frustration. He often withdraws from further overtures toward a significant relationship with Mom and Dad.

We don't mean to imply that *all* teenagers will automatically respond to reasonable, warm persuasion. Some teens are so enmeshed in the struggles of adolescence that they bristle at *any* parental approach. The only answer is to keep trying to reach them and to pray.

Parental self-control assumes major importance in communications during the teen years. If the teenager expects an angry, vitriolic response, he isn't likely to initiate a conversation. 1 Corinthians 13:4-7 gives us key principles to use with anyone, and especially with our teenagers.

> Love is patient, love is kind. It does not envy, it does not boast, it is not proud. It is not rude, it is not self-seeking, it is not easily angered, it keeps no record of wrongs. Love does not delight in evil but rejoices with the truth. It always protects, always trusts, always hopes, always perseveres.

Do your children recognize these attitudes in you?

When one of our daughters was in high school she said, "Whenever I talk about boys, I can tell by your faces what you are thinking. You are wondering what he is like, and why I'm talking about him. You don't even wait to hear what I am going to say. I'm not going to talk about it any more." We had to apologize, and begin again, realizing that her relationships with boys were natural, and we were fortunate she wanted to talk with us about them.

A look can delay or cancel proper communication. We need to keep our expressions neutral or positive when our children share with us, expressing only genuine interest in what they say. A look of disgust, fear, apprehension, disapproval, or disbelief will sever effective communication. We have found some suggestions helpful in communicating with teens.[2]

- Be courteous.
- Expect and require courtesy from them.
- Listen when they are ready to talk.
- Hear them out before responding.
- Give them your *full* attention.
- Sympathize with them in their struggles.

Independence. As teenagers mature they must move toward independence in all areas of life. Here are a few suggestions to help them do this.

1. Allow increasing freedom. Teenagers will make mistakes and poor decisions. But it is much better for that to happen when we can still offer help and advice than when they have left home. Encourage them to make their own decisions and support them to the fullest.
2. Welcome other influences. When our children are young, we are the most important people in their lives. But the time will come when we cannot be all things to our children. As they approach adulthood, others may step in to fill a gap that we can no longer fill.

   When our son was in high school, two men strongly influenced him in a positive, spiritual way. One was a high school teacher, the other a youth worker at church. These men shared two common characteristics—a genuine interest in Steve and an acceptance of him as he was with a view toward his potential.

The contributing person may be a godly friend, relative, teacher, counselor, youth pastor, or Christian neighbor. Any positive spiritual input during the teen years enriches their lives and your own relationship with them.

3. Be a friend, not a buddy. Teenagers don't need or want parents who look and talk like them. We are adults. We must be our mature selves to give them a solid pattern to follow. A friend allows for weaknesses and idiosyncrasies but still accepts the person. Accept their friends. Respect their privacy. Give them your time. Pray for them.

4. Limit criticism and increase approval. Someone has said that parents criticize nine times for every time they praise their child, and yet it takes four commendations to offset one criticism. During the emotionally fragile years of adolescence, we must positively reinforce our children's self-images. They need to hear our spoken appreciation, approval, and pride as often as possible. We have opportunities to build their self-images at a time when their peers and their environment would tear them down.

What have you said today to increase your teenager's respect for himself? Have you shared anything that would build him up, or has your conversation left him feeling defeated and rejected? "A man finds joy in giving an apt reply—and how good is a timely word!" (Proverbs 15:23).

Enjoy your teenagers. They leave quickly. Minimize

your own mid-life struggles and maximize the opportunities to know and appreciate your own children.

No set of rules or suggestions can prevent the inevitable teen/parent conflicts. An awareness of our need to not neglect them and to understand both them and our reactions to them will help us. Whatever the history of your relationship with your teens, it is not too late for it to improve!

Paul said, "I press on toward the goal" (Philippians 3:14). He did not say, "I dwell on my past." We now have the great privilege of changing roles from parent to friend, from control to counsel, and from directing to praying. The move to an adult relationship does not happen overnight. It must be nurtured and built over a period of time. Adolescence will pass. Maturity will come, though not always in the precise way we would have designed. Our children are not the same as us. They have their own lives to live and their own talents to give. Our task is to help them find their greatest fulfillment in both their spiritual and their physical life.

May God grant us the patience and wisdom to act toward our teenage children as mature, spiritual, adults living under the control of the Holy Spirit.

Tagalongs

Mary was almost thirty-five when our fourth child was born. Judy married at thirty-five and had her first baby at thirty-six. The Smiths had two children in college and one in high school when a baby girl arrived. John and Carol were told she could never conceive. When she was forty-two, she became pregnant.

Few mid-life events are as surprising as the arrival of a

baby. The birth of an infant seems incongruous, so out of place, so inconvenient! The parents have to adjust dramatically. Many lifestyle changes must be made. Although this is not a common occurrence, we observe enough "tagalongs" to warrant a few comments regarding this major mid-life event.

We face many issues when a pregnancy occurs in mid-life.

Your Response

Disbelief. "Oh no. Our son is engaged to be married next year!" "Why it can't be! I'm forty-two!" "Oh, my goodness! It's like Sarah in the Bible!" "Pregnant! We're so old!" "A baby! At our age? Ridiculous!"

By mid-life we have established a routine which doesn't readily accommodate an infant. When we face that prospect, our minds balk at the magnitude of the changes we must make.

Resentment. A baby disturbs an established schedule. Someone said, "It's like throwing a monkey wrench into a well-oiled machine." A baby increases the workload. A child born in the mid-years restricts parents well into later life. Unless we recognize the source of resentment as personal selfishness and deal with it, that attitude will spill over and ruin our relationship with the child.

Embarrassment. The question, "What will people say?" plays a part in determining our attitudes toward the child. Christian parents need to ignore the questions and comments of curious or critical family members and friends and accept the baby as another welcome, God-given member of the family.

Emotional stress. By mid-life we feel we have passed the point where we can accept the emotional bombardment of living with a preschooler. They are constantly on the go, they're inexhaustible, noisy, and messy. They turn order into chaos and ruin any semblance of tranquility. Surely a person in middle age can't handle that.

Inflexibility. In mid-life the intrusion of a child forces change. We don't want to change. We don't appreciate the pressure. We don't feel like adapting. After all, we were comfortable and orderly. Suddenly we are forced to cast that routine aside and accept something new and difficult. Although these feelings commonly arise when raising a child later in life, we have found the blessings can far outweigh the adjustments.

Many people equate an unwanted pregnancy with an unwanted child. But God allows enough time for us to prepare our hearts and homes for a child, however inconvenient and unexpected. Psalm 127:3 remains true regardless of the parents' age when the child is born. "Sons are a heritage from the Lord, children a reward from him," even in mid life.

Children are God's gifts to us, even in mid-life. Often children born in our maturity provide a living rebuke to our initial reactions of resentment and rejection. They can bring so much joy, love, and laughter into our homes.

Remember the story of Elizabeth and Zechariah recorded in Luke 1? They were middle-aged, but the son God gave them proved a source of pride to them and spiritual blessing to his generation.

Susanna Wesley bore nineteen children between her twenty-first and fortieth birthdays. Two of her children contributed significantly to the Christian world and their influence is still felt today. Susanna was thirty when John Wesley was born and thirty-nine when Charles Wesley was born. No doubt she longed for a respite from children as she aged. But God chose to bless her with sons who had a spiritual impact for centuries.

God may give you a child he will use significantly. Or your child may be quite ordinary. Either way, they remain precious in God's sight and deserve the best love, care, and training you can provide.

How to Cope and Like It

Get God's perspective. Give thanks to God daily for your child. Express appreciation to the Lord for allowing you the privilege of raising that particular child. Pray daily for wisdom in parenting. Even though you may have raised other children, you probably still have much to learn. Renew your understanding of the biblical concepts of child rearing.

Willingly adjust your schedule. Life must necessarily change with the advent of a child in mid-life. Determine to change gracefully. Some activities will have to be eliminated. Children present restrictions. Accept them and adjust willingly.

Be consistent in training. After the initial shock of pregnancy wears off, and God replaces resentment with anticipation, we may be so delighted that the child is treated as a favored pet, almost reverenced by the proud parents. Disobedience and nastiness sometimes seem insignificant and even cute. We tend to ignore the need for correction. We thus do the child an injustice. God has given us an opportunity to use our accumulated wisdom to give the child a consistent, thorough training. Let's not deny him the right to our loving, steady discipline and correction.

Don't let them run your life. If you permit their whims to dictate to you, you will destroy normalcy in your home. Parents must be in charge and it's to the child's advantage to experience and observe your authority.

When our daughter was born, our son was entering

adolescence, a time when boys seem compelled to prove their toughness by recoiling from hugs, kisses, and words of love. But he could demonstrate his natural tenderness toward a baby without any loss of face.

A baby was born with Down's syndrome in a large family of our acquaintance. The entire family rallied around that little one with love and protection.

Having a young child around during our mid-years keeps us youthful. Or, as one weary mother said, "If it didn't keep you young, you would age twice as fast." We must mold our thinking to their concerns and interests. Once again we can view the world through a child's eyes.

Because of these younger children, we can maintain contacts and friendships with younger parents. Our children provide ready access to families in the neighborhood through their playmates. Many Christian parents of mid-life babies have led young couples to Christ because they became acquainted as their children played together.

Never feel intimidated because you are the oldest parents crouching on tiny chairs watching a nursery school program. Don't feel embarrassed if your age outstrips all others at the local Parent-Teachers' Associaton. You can still maintain, enjoy, and profit from those contacts and opportunities.

A younger child gives older children an opportunity to experience responsibility. One mother who had a baby girl when her daughter was sixteen said, "My older daughter's high school friend had a baby. She tried to explain to my daughter how terrific it was to have a baby, but since we already had a baby at home, my daughter knew that much responsibility comes with the fun. She knows from firsthand observation the effort as well as the joys of having a baby in the house."

Grandchildren

"By the time the youngest children have learned to keep the place tidy, the oldest grandchildren are at hand to tear it up."[3]

It is in God's plan that grandparents have a significant influence on their grandchildren. This becomes even more important if the grandparents know the Lord and are walking with him.

God's word exhorts grandparents to "only be careful, and watch yourselves closely so that you do not forget the things your eyes have seen or let them slip from your heart as long as you live. Teach them to your children and to their children after them" (Deuteronomy 4:9). Further instruction is given in Deuteronomy 6:1-2.

> These are the commands, decrees and laws the Lord your God directed me to teach you to observe in the land that you are crossing the Jordan to possess, so that you, your children and their children after them may fear the Lord your God as long as you live by keeping all his decrees and commands that I give you, and so that you may enjoy long life.

Grandparenting brings special years of joy. Grandparents feel the freedom to boast about the exceptional qualities of their grandchildren. As parents they were restrained by the fear of pride, but not as grandparents. They readily share the amazing progress and feats of their grandchildren. They display numerous pictures. They love to show admiring friends their grandchildren. And they secretly question the intelligence of anyone who fails to immediately recognize how extraordinary their grandchild is.

But with all of the joys come certain responsibilities.

If there has been a break in the relationship with your married children, the arrival of grandchildren will present an opportunity for restoration and healing. Just as a family rallies in love and harmony around a late arriving child, so too can grandparents and their children develop a new understanding and relationship over the shared joy of a newly arrived baby.

Because the child is a grandchild, grandparents need to keep certain things clearly in mind. Grandpa and Grandma are *not* responsible before the Lord for raising that child. The parents bear full responsibility, and while grandparents enhance a child's life, they do not direct it. Interference by grandparents can quickly cause wounded feelings, bruised relationships, and long-lasting resentments.

We spoke with a woman at a conference who was livid with indignation. During the conference she had called home to find that Grandmother, who was watching the children, had forced her twelve-year-old girl to have her hair cut, against the girl's wishes and without the parents' permission. In that case Grandmother had just ruined her relationship, and her influence for some time to come, with that family.

Grandparents need to be cautious about interfering. New parents are sensitive about their inexperience and keenly aware of their mistakes. They resent advice and instrusion. Grandparents have an unparalleled opportunity to pray for their grandchildren, and watch God work in their lives. If they see mistakes and misjudgment in the parenting, grandparents need to ask God to step in. The only exception would be if the child were being harmed or abused in any way. Then direct intervention would be warranted.

Grandparents need to restrain open disapproval of

their grandchildren or the way they are being raised. A cutting remark will remain in the parents' memory for years. If you feel like saying, "Good grief, you're spoiling that child," restrain yourself. Open criticism gains nothing and may merely alienate your children.

Grandparents need to avoid countering parental standards. If you feel that the parents are too strict, don't undermine the directives the parents have given. If they say the child can't have candy before meals, don't give him any. If a son or daughter must be in by eleven o'clock on weekends, don't invite him to your home and let him stay out until one in the morning. Parents have the right and the responsibility to set the standards by which their children live, and grandparents must respect those stadards.

Some grandparents display indifference to their grandchildren. Perhaps they feel they are too young to really be traditional grandparents, or maybe they live some distance from the children and don't take the time to correspond. Or perhaps they are extremely busy or just don't care. Indifference communicates a keen rejection to children and grandchildren alike. Make every effort to keep close ties with your grandchildren even if there is little response.

Grandparents can exert a strong influence on their grandchildren, and God expects that.

Pray for them. Perhaps no one else in the world prays for your grandchildren but you. God will certainly hear your prayers. Perhaps your children are living apart from God and their children receive no spiritual training. Pray for your grandchildren and influence them where you can.

A grandmother we know has two grandsons. She is a fine Christian woman. Her daughter received spiritual training as a growing girl, but rejected that training during her university years. When she married and had children, she forbid her mother to speak to them about the things of God. For years that grandmother prayed for her grandchildren and watched them grow up without any spiritual training. When the oldest grandson graduated from high school and reached the age of eighteen she told him, "My dear, there has been something missing in your education. now that you are a young man I would like to tell you what it is." And she proceeded to give him the gospel that he had not heard in his own home.

Reinforce parental teaching. If your grandchildren are living in a Christian home, you can contribute to their lives by reinforcing and demonstrating the same values in your home that they see in theirs. Let them hear you pray. Occasionally give them gifts that have spiritual significance. Our own children have been greatly enriched because they have seen their grandparents' dedication to the Lord.

Be an elder counselor. Perhaps your grandchildren's Mom and Dad are busy, discouraged, or problem-oriented. You may be able to offer understanding, care, and acceptance. Most people can quickly point out their parents' negative qualities, but remember their grandparents with kindness and warmth. That is because grandparents have the chance to influence without enforcing unwelcome restrictions. Take advantage of your position and foster the love and respect of your grandchildren.

Here are some guidelines for properly relating to the two younger generations:

- Be honest with your children. If you can't babysit, or don't want to, say so. If you find that their children don't meet the standards you expect in your home, say so. But again, be wary of personal criticisms.
- Love the grandchildren and leave them alone. Don't

interfere or fret. Worry won't change any situation. Pray instead.

- Influence by example. Jerry's grandmother stayed with us for several weeks when our first-born was a toddler. She saw mistakes we made but never said a word. Instead, she showed us a better way. We caught on quickly and our relationship never suffered because of open criticism, although it was probably warranted.

- Don't demand time. Your grandchildren may have full schedules and can't always accommodate your wishes for seeing them frequently. If your feelings are hurt confess it to the Lord, but not to your children.

- Don't invade the privacy of your children's homes. They have a need to develop a family structure and style of their own. It may be well to wait for an invitation before visiting them. At least call to check their schedule before dropping by unexpectedly. What if you live with them? Make every attempt to fit in with their plans and to contribute to their pattern of life.

God gives grandchildren as an evidence of his blessing, as a sign of the continuity of life, and as a joy in old age. Welcome them and respond to the joys they bring. We always enjoy seeing the bumper sticker, "Ask me about my grandbaby." Wouldn't it be great to see a bumper sticker that said, "Ask me about my grandparents"? That will be the attitude of our grandchildren if we take our grandparenting task seriously.

NOTES: 1. *Webster's New Collegiate Dictionary,* (Springfield, Massachusetts: G. & C. Merriam Company, 1973), page 1352.
2. Haim Ginott, *Between Parent and Teenager,* (New York: Macmillan Company, 1969).
3. *The International Encyclopedia of Thoughts,* (Chicago: J. G. Ferguson Publishing House, 1975), page 127.

CHAPTER 9

Singleness in Mid-life

"Singleness is a gift to be accepted, used, and enjoyed. If my loving heavenly Father, who only gives good and perfect gifts, has given me the gift of singleness, I can accept it, and by an act of the will I can commit myself to fulfilling his purposes for my short span of life here on earth—or for however long God sees fit for me to remain single.

"The single life is an opportunity. Single men and women never had it so good. Singleness is more accepted than ever as a viable lifestyle. As a single woman, I am free to do things many married women cannot or should not do. I am free to attend to the Lord without distraction.

"Is a single woman missing something by not being married? Yes! But who has everything in this world? Few marriages come close to the ideal. With the joy of marriage also come responsibilities which I don't have to face.

"Also, I am thankful that I am not:

- a wife forsaken by divorce
- a widow bereaved by her husband's death
- a heartbroken mother of a rebellious child"[1]

The United States census bureau has reported revealing statistics regarding the single population in our country. In a report entitled "Marital Status and Living Arrangements" some new facts were disclosed.

As of March, 1978, more than one American household in five consisted of someone living as a single. According to the report, 62 percent of the single-person households were maintained by women, although since 1970 the proportion of men living alone has grown more rapidly than the women's percentage. In 1970 the Bureau reported 47 divorced persons for every 1,000 married individuals in the United States. By 1978 this number had grown 91 percent to 90 divorced persons for every 1,000 who remained married.[2]

Whether you are single because of death, divorce, or by personal choice, you are in a rapidly growing portion of our society. This trend also proves true in the Christian community.

Some characteristics of the single life make it unique. There are advantages and disadvantages not experienced by couples. Let's consider some of the advantages.

Advantages of Being Single

The Apostle Paul wrote specifically on this topic.

> Now to the unmarried and the widows I say: It is good for them to stay unmarried, as I am. . . .I would like you to be free from concern. An unmarried man is concerned about the Lord's affairs—how he can please the Lord. . . .An unmarried woman or virgin is concerned about the Lord's affairs: Her aim is to be

devoted to the Lord in both body and spirit. But a
married woman is concerned about the affairs of this
world—how she can please her husband. I am saying
this for your own good, not to restrict you, but that
you may live in a right way in undivided devotion to
the Lord (1 Corinthians 7:8, 32, and 34-35).

Paul summed up this teaching in 1 Corinthians 7:17.
"Nevertheless, each one should retain the place in life that
the Lord assigned to him and to which God has called
him." Most people marry. The assumption that marriage
is best for everyone seems natural. But that is not
necessarily so, as Paul points out in 1 Corinthians 7. Paul
authenticates singleness as a biblically acceptable lifestyle.

Freedom for Career Changes

When single people decide to move or make major
career changes, the responsibilities and needs of a family
do not stop them. Their mobility facilitates rapid relo-
cation. Their finances can be cut drastically, if need be, to
allow for retraining or a move. This is not to say singles do
not have roots and restrictions. While singles do have
associations and interests, friends and ties, they are more
mobile than married people.

One man we know travels extensively in his work.
Every few years he leaves his job for a year or so, to do further research or study. During those times he lives frugally
on a portion of the savings he set aside while working. He
has never owned a home or a car. His possessions can be
packed in a few boxes. But his expertise in his career field
is vast. He never fails to find work quickly when his personal sabbaticals end. Certainly such an unusual lifestyle
would have been much more complex, or impossible, if he
had been married. He, of course, is an exception and his

lifestyle is unusual even for a single. Not every single person would care to opt for such an unorthodox pattern of life. Most will follow a traditional pattern of education and employment. But when opportunities for change come, a single person can act quickly and easily.

This may not be quite so true if children are involved following a divorce or the death of a spouse. However, even children do not limit a decision in the same way a marriage partner would. Children adapt readily to new situations and locations.

Less Complex Lifestyle

- Possessions can be discarded or ignored. Singles can choose a small apartment rather than a large condominium or house. Many choose to invest in a house, but aren't forced to do so because of family size.
- Friends are chosen and cherished without concern for a mate's approval.
- Finances generally cover the needs of one adult.
- Extended family relationships involve fewer people. In-laws don't exist in the same way as for marrieds. Even divorced and widowed people with children have fewer complications.
- Singles are free from parenting responsibilities.

Control of Time

Single people have to consider only one person when scheduling their time. Only one set of activities, and one sphere of relationships are involved.

Single people can more readily add or delete activities because they are not as limited by or responsible for the lives and involvements with immediate family members as marrieds would be. When planning a week's schedule, singles need not consult mate and children in order to plan.

Even though a roommate shares the home, their time restrictions differ from a family. Babies do not disturb at three a.m. No baby-sitter is needed. You are not locked into someone else's schedule.

As a single, you can choose activities and responsibilities which restrict you as much as a married person. But it is your choice, not a necessity.

Freedom to Serve God

The apostle Paul understood the advantages of being single and free to serve God. He specifically mentioned "undivided devotion to the Lord" (1 Corinthians 7:35). Single people have the advantage of being free to serve the Lord without family requirements pressing upon them.

The Old Testament heroine Ruth told Naomi, "Don't urge me to leave you or to turn back from you. Where you go I will go, and where you stay I will stay. Your people will be my people and your God my God" (Ruth 1:16). Ruth was free to make radical changes in her location and lifestyle because she was single.

Mary's stepmother served God for twenty-five years on the mission field. She experienced high adventure with God as she saw him provide her needs: protection, companionship, comfort, finances, health, and friends. God gave her a young girl from an extremely poor family to care for and educate. She saw many spiritual victories won, and many people came to Christ because of her service on the mission field.

Stories abound of men and women who remained single, or who married late in life, who devoted their lives to serving God in a full-time capacity. Men and women like Amy Carmichael in India, J.O. Fraser in China's interior, and Henrietta Mears who taught at First Presbyterian Church in Hollywood, California, are a few of those who have served God faithfully while single.

In 1976 single men and women represented 32.1 percent of the total American overseas missionary force (counting a couple as one unit). Single women composed 26.9 percent of the total.[3] In spite of much controversy and discussion about the role of women in the church, women (and especially single women) have made an outstanding contribution to the cause of world missions. Single women responded to God's call when many others did not.

On the other hand, many single men and women who were called to missions or full-time service, decided to marry someone who did not share their call or desire to serve God. Many chose marriage to non-Christians or immature Christians and blunted their contribution to the cause of Christ.

Most single people will maintain a lifestyle in the traditional manner—with a career, a home, friends, and an extended family. But because of their limited immediate family commitments, they will be more free to serve God in various roles. As Sunday school teachers they never need to miss because they have sick children at home. They can more freely devote an evening to leading Bible studies or ministering to the ill, the elderly, or young people. If God calls them to minister in another culture, they can do so with less financial support than a family and will get along with simpler travel and living arrangements.

Our son was strongly and positively influenced during his high school years by a single, middle-aged Christian teacher who had time available to take boys mountain climbing and teach them how to rappel. Through sports he demonstrated godly care and concern for those boys at a time when such an influence was greatly needed. During the adolescent years the influence of parents needs bolstering by other godly adults. God can effectively use singles in many areas:

- youth work
- teaching Sunday school
- counseling youth
- discipling
- travel ministries
- short-term foreign missions

Some singles who have reached mid-life may want to consider a fresh avenue of service to God. If you have not or are not now making a contribution to the Body of Christ, consider where you could invest your life. You will first want to discover your areas of interest and your spiritual gifts. If you do not know your spiritual gifts, counsel with a godly friend or your pastor. Then resolve to begin making a contribution to the Body of Christ. You have much to offer.

Disadvantages of Being Single

Loneliness

There is a loneliness that defies description for some singles. When they experience joys or sorrows, they have no close companion with whom to share. If they are sick, discouraged, or depressed, unless they have a close friend, they must bear that burden alone.

By mid-life many single people recognize they may remain single for the rest of their lives, and they fear the loneliness that they may face. Many single women have no close friend with whom they can share the details of their stresses and problems. It is important for single women to develop strong relationships with another woman or a couple who can give counsel and caring friendship. Man also need similar, close relationships.

Financial Problems

Single women, especially in mid-life, recognize that unless they have an exceptional job, they will always live on the lean side of financial success. Most women still do not make an amount of money equivalent to what most men would make for comparable jobs. It can be frightening to look into a future where retirement benefits will be their only buffer between poverty and an adequate standard of living if no family exists to care for them.

It is a heavy responsibility to be your only source of support, provide solely for yourself since ill health or losing your job could destroy your financial security. As Christians we recognize that God is our provider and all good things come from him. But somehow our paycheck becomes the evidence of God's provision, and we find it hard to believe that he could provide for us in any other way.

Our tax structure, while slowly changing, still favors married people, and those responsible for the financial welfare of others. It is aggravating to see a seminar advertised for $14 per person or $25 per couple, or to go to the grocery store and find only two-pound packages of hamburger when all you need is a half-pound.

Sexual Pressures

Singleness does not eliminate sexuality. In 1 Corinthians 7 Paul urged those who were unable to control their feelings to marry. But what of those who never have such an opportunity? How does the single person handle the desire for sexual fulfillment and attraction to another?

Unless single people are convinced from God's word that immorality is sin, they can easily be swayed by prevailing attitudes which favor freely satisfying sexual needs outside the marriage bond. Restraint is not a popular concept.

The answer to sexual desire is not repression, but redirection by using that energy in creative, useful, and helpful ways. That is, sexual expression in a biblical sense is based on a giving, loving feeling. If God has not given you a mate for life, then use that available loving force to extend yourself to others in some caring, helpful way. Immorality, homosexuality, idle flirtations, and masturbation are not the answer. But active helpful involvement in the lives of others will give permanent release to the loving nature that cries out for expression and satisfaction.

Short-term physical release can also be obtained through consistent and vigorous physical exercise. It is wise to maintain good health. It is also helpful to avoid stimulating films, television programs, and reading material.

Many men and women who have been married and are now divorced or widowed must carefully guard their sexual drives. Because of past experience, they will be more aware of the lack of sexual expression in their lives. They have a strong memory basis for fantasy, mental indiscretions, and physical drives. But while single, the sexual needs and desires are to be brought under control and channeled, regardless of past experience. Restraint and self-discipline are two hallmarks of the Christian life. God does not make these requirements to cause struggle and pain, but rather so that our lives, under the control of the Holy Spirit, will glorify him.

Sexual indiscretions and promiscuity by Christians, perhaps more than any other activity, can quickly bring disrepute on the reputation of God. Of course, this applies to all Christians, married or single. But those who were once married, and are now single, are called upon to demonstrate a control that will involve both the mind and the body. A similar problem exists for singles who were sexually promiscuous in the past, but who now wish to be obedient to God in the area of purity.

Selfishness

Singles can develop patterns of living that easily exclude others and develop habits of self-indulgence and selfishness. It is easy to become self-centered and unwilling to share time, money, and possessions. Such actions may be based on right motives, which simply took the wrong form of expression.

A middle-aged single woman may refuse to give generously to her church, feeling that she needs to reserve extra finances for her future. Another may refuse to participate in church or community because she thinks, "I'm just one person and I don't make any demands on anyone. Why should they make demands on me?"

The Apostle Paul wrote in Philippians 2:4, "Each of you should look not only to your own interests, but also to the interests of others."

Be careful that a solitary lifestyle does not result in a selfish mode of living. Combat such a threat by extending yourself to others, making it known that you are available and ready to participate unselfishly in the lives of others.

The Body of Christ is richer for the contribution of single people. Make certain that you do not deprive others in the Body of what God has given you to share.

Resentment and Bitterness

"I came from a family of five sisters," one woman

told us. "They're all married with children of their own. I even have nieces and nephews who are married. I'm forty-five now. I know I'll never get married. Deep down inside I'm angry—furious really—that God didn't give me a husband. Why did I have to be the one to stay single?"

The Apostle Paul understood the devastation that bitterness can produce personally and communally. He wrote the Ephesians, "Get rid of all bitterness, rage and anger" (Ephesians 4:31). The author of Hebrews wrote, "See to it that no one misses the grace of God and that no bitter root grows up to cause trouble and defile many" (Hebrews 12:15).

Men and women who desired marriage but reached mid-life without a mate must carefully guard against bitterness and resentment. For bitterness is not a solitary emotion. Eventually it distorts an individual's entire personality and then spreads outward to those around him. Bitterness destroys joy, productivity, and happiness. The answer to bitterness is a confidence in God's good purpose for you and a thankful spirit. It is difficult to remain bitter while constantly thanking God.

Inflexibility

Because the single's lifestyle presents the opportunity to live without considering the requirements of others, singles face the danger of becoming inflexible. This becomes truer in mid-life, not only for the singles but for marrieds as well. A refusal to change schedules, personality quirks, and set patterns of thinking can lead to an individual's becoming set in concrete.

It is vital to remain flexible, however, to be a learner throughout life. Being flexible combines responding sensitively to the needs of others and to the aspects of our own lives that should change. We should daily ask God to point out to us, through the inner working of the Holy Spirit and through his word, those things that are rigid and unproductive in our lives. We need to ask God to show us how we can change. And we need to be open to any suggestions and counsel others may have about the negative aspects of our lives.

Christian Curiosity

To many singles, especially those who have never been married, one of the most irritating aspects of singleness is the curiosity of their Christian brothers and sisters.

- "I can't understand why you aren't married.
- "You are such a wonderful person. Surely someone would like to marry you."
- "My cousin will be in town Friday. She's single and I know you would love to meet her."
- "Has anyone ever asked you to marry?"
- "If you would be just a little more aggressive, you would be married in no time."

Christian singles are quick to point out that Christians are often far less tolerant of the single life than is the secular world. One Christian woman told us, "Perhaps it is because they are happily married and want us to join them. But I think it is more likely that they can't comprehend that a single person can be satisfied and fulfilled. It's possible, but they refuse to believe it."

Many Christians need to understand that God will call some to a single life. Even so, singles who are still praying and trusting God for a life partner will not appreciate constant probing into their unmarried state. It will be much easier for them to remain content and satisfied with their single life if married people would stop interfering.

Enjoying the Single Life

Recognize God's Sovereignty

God knows each person's need and works for their good. If he chooses the single life for you, he knows that is best. A sense of relaxation and freedom comes when you trust God's perfect sovereignty and will concerning the choice of a married life or a single life.

The key to a joyous life, whether single or married, is the right relationship with God. Many singles feel that life would be enhanced if only they were married. Many married people think life would improve if only they were single again, so they proceed to divorce their mates. However, marital status doesn't offer the key to a happy life—only peace with God does. The apostle Paul emphasized this.

> Nevertheless, each one should retain the place in life that the Lord assigned to him and to which God has called him. . .Keeping God's commands is what counts. . . .Brothers, each man, as responsible to God, should remain in the situation God called him to (1 Corinthians 7:7, 19, 24).

Many singles waste much of their time and emotions living for a future that may never come. They keep trusting, hoping, and praying that God will give them a mate, all the while missing the joy of being single and walking daily in rich fellowship with God.

Is your life filled with questions? Do you keep reminding God of your desire for a life partner? Do you feel you have waited long enough? Or do you thank and praise God for your singleness? Are you living to the fullest now? Are you leaving your future in his hands?

Appreciate Your Singleness

Accepting singleness lays a foundation for a fulfilled life. But appreciating and thanking God for singleness builds the superstructure of a completed and whole life. If God has given you the gift of being single, recognize it as such. It is not God's second best. It is the very best life God could design for you. Live in the present. Reject the waste of pining for marriage. If God eventually brings a mate, thank him. If you are to remain single, by God's grace be the most joyous single person you can be.

It would be simple if our society didn't emphasize marriage so much. But we assume that being single is temporary until the right partner comes along. So many people live with a transitory feeling that the single period of their lives will be brief. For most, that will be so. But how healthy it would be if all singles could live confidently without feeling pressured to look toward a future that God may not have planned.

We all need to arrive at a point where we verbally commit ourselves to God and his plan for our lives, whether that means marriage or a single life. Until we reach that point of commitment, we will always be restless, reaching for the future, and dissatisfied with life.

If you are single and your life goal has been marriage, then you will experience frustration and disappointment because you haven't achieved your goals. But if your goals are godly living and making a contribution to others' lives, you can pursue them vigorously throughout life whether married or single.

On a quiet afternoon or evening, try this exercise. With paper and pen review all the reasons you appreciate being single. Jot down all the advantages you can think of. If you have readily adapted to the life God has chosen for you, you should easily be able to think of a dozen items.

Consider these advantages:

- I can live and work where I choose.
- I can plan meals I enjoy or not cook at all.
- No one regularly interrupts my quiet times with God.
- I can vacation wherever I want to.
- I can serve God anywhere.
- I can choose an apartment or a house I like and decorate it as I choose.
- I can trust God to be my companion and comfort.
- I can read for half the night without bothering anyone.

Focus on the privilege of walking with God and seeing him provide your needs and enrich your life.

Develop Strong Friendships

Single people need friends, especially if they do not have a roommate, or members of their family nearby. Close friends provide a buffer against loneliness. They can offer counsel and advice and provide companionship for shared activities. "A man that hath friends must shew himself friendly: and there is a friend that sticketh closer than a brother" (Proverbs 18:24 KJV).

Any relationship takes time. But the investment of time is repaid with the satisfaction of knowing another person and receiving and giving friendship and love. For single people, friendship is important because a healthy life is one filled with relationships with people. In marriage situations certain relationships are mandatory. But singles can choose the relationships they want to develop.

Take the time to make friends. All relationships naturally require making oneself vulnerable to hurt as well as happiness. We need to understand that for a friendship to be strong, it will experience some ups and downs. But friendships that have gone through such times have been strengthened by them, and they will remain fresh and renewed for years to come.

Some single people in mid-life will have roommates or housemates for social or financial reasons. But a roommate does not automatically become a friend. If you do live with someone, try to select an individual who is congenial and compatible with your personality. Then cultivate a friendship as you would with anyone else. Friendship takes time, tolerance, and understanding. Make an effort to keep your living situation functional, but harmonious. A roommate can be a counselor and a companion, but it will not happen merely because you live in the same house or apartment. A quality relationship develops only after much time, energy, and consideration have been invested. Singles, like marrieds, need small groups in which they are accountable to their peers and in which they receive the love, support, and encouragement of other Christian singles.

Nieces and Nephews

Most single people will have nieces and nephews. One of the great contributions they can make is to influence the lives of those growing children. They can provide a godly model, offer counsel that might not be accepted from parents, and provide a sympathetic, listening ear.

Our children have an aunt, Ruth Knutson, who has done just that for them. She listens to them, laughs with them, never appears hurried or rushed (as we too often do), sings with them, and has influenced them by her dedication to the Lord. She has established some traditions that they look forward to as an evidence of her interest and concern for them. She takes each of them to breakfast on their birthday; she never forgets a Christmas gift. She has taught our daughters about fashion. She has taught them music. They know she is dependable, concerned, and available. She is able to influence and enjoy them without having to exercise restrictions, discipline, and correction. Our family has been enriched by her contribution to their lives as a single woman.

If you have nieces and nephews, review your relationships with them and determine how you could make a more effective impact on their lives. Incidentally, you will be cultivating and enriching your relationship with their parents. For what parents aren't pleased when their children receive constructive attention?

Make a Home

Many single people assume that they will soon be married. However, if marriage hasn't taken place by mid-life, the possibility is reduced. If you are still living with a "temporary" feeling, you are missing the experience of establishing a home of your own.

Accept your singleness as permanent. Decide what kind of a home you would like. Then establish such a place for yourself. It may be a tiny, one-room apartment, or a house in the suburbs. Determine before God what you will use your home for. Could it be a place of ministry? Could you invite others there for spiritual fellowship and restoration? What do you personally enjoy in a home? Determine how you can make it a haven, a place of rest and relaxation.

Use your home to serve the Lord. It need not be elaborate, but it must be a welcoming place, and that will depend on you, not the decor. Let others know that you freely share your home and want them to enjoy it with you. Invite others for meals or for an evening of fellowship. Use your home for hospitality, Bible studies, group gatherings, counseling, and prayer.

Mary and Martha, the sisters described in Luke 10:30-42, were evidently single, but they used their home to provide a place for refreshment and rest for the Lord and his disciples. Mary and Martha were both dedicated to learning from him, and used their home for that purpose also.

So you're single in mid-life. Thank God. Accept the best that God has for you. Live today without straining toward tomorrow. Allow God to use your life in a productive, unique way. Continue to grow in him and to experience the work of the Holy Spirit in your life. Live happily without embarrassment or apology for your single state, recognizing that it is God's best for you. Make it your goal to live a full, godly life, and allow God to use you in any way he sees fit.

NOTES: 1. Millie Hopkins, in a speech given at Glen Eyrie, Navigator Headquarters, Colorado Springs, Colorado, May, 1978.
2. "Single Life-style Is Changing the Housing Market," *The Seattle Times,* July 26, 1978, page F3.
3. Edward R. Dayton, editor, *Mission Handbook: North American Protestant Ministries Overseas* (Monrovia, California: Missions Advanced Research and Communications Center, 1977).

CHAPTER 10

Ruts, Roots, and Recreation

He sat with his jaw set, tight lips, and a grim face. For the past year Phil had been upset over the changes taking place in his church. No doctrinal problem, he admitted, but minor changes that simply rubbed him the wrong way. For a while he reacted philosophically, but now it was getting to him. He liked the church the way it was. He resisted the changes, but was unable to prevent them. He often abstained on votes at church board meetings. Inwardly he churned. Soon he felt awkward with even his good friends. Finally disagreement over an insignificant issue caused his family to leave the church.

Inflexibility, ruts, and an unwillingness to change,—a kind of arthritis of the mind—are some of the major problems of mid-life. These, along with other characteristic issues of mid-life are discussed in this chapter.

Inflexibility

Solidifying our ideas, beliefs, and goals is a sign of maturity. Prejudice should not be confused with mature conviction. At one extreme is the brittleness of inflexibility which paralyzes a person and prevents growth and new ideas. At the other extreme is the person who has no convictions at all, and responds to every wind of change. Neither extreme is desirable.

Inflexibility is most likely to develop as we grow older. We are tired of the years of discovery and experimentation. We develop a liking for order and routine. So many changes are already at work in our lives. We don't want more change.

Yet change we must. Change and development are the foundation stones for growth. Change relates to every area of life—intellectual, physical, social, and spiritual.

At age seventy-five Eric Hoffer, the workingman's philosopher of this century, commented, "To become really mature is to return to the age of five, to be able to recapture the capacity for absorption, for learning, to recapture the tremendous hunger to master skills that you had at five."[1] We must not lose our ability to learn and change. If you find yourself resenting and resisting change, take it as a warning that you may be losing your flexibility. The body certainly becomes less supple with age, but the mind can continue to grow and respond. The Scriptures teach that we are "better poor, but wise youth than an old but foolish king who no longer knows how to take warning" (Ecclesiastes 4:13). Maturity and discipleship are processes of constant learning and development.

In your marriage, your work, your spiritual growth, and your interpersonal relationships, the ability to respond positively to change is one of your greatest assets. We do not mean that you should violate principles of Scripture for the sake of change, but simply that you allow God to change you. God, in his sovereignty, places us in the midst of change.

What can you do to train yourself to respond in a godly way? First, review the past few months to see if you have responded badly to some change. If so, identify the specific areas where you regularly resist change. Pinpoint your inflexible areas and begin to do specific things to break out of the pattern. When you react negatively to something different, ask yourself whether your reaction stems from a scriptural principle or from personal preference.

One of the greatest ways to be challenged to change is spending extended time with teenagers or young adults. Listen to them. Think about what they are saying and doing. Let them challenge the way your family lives. Finally, purposefully develop a "change-a-month" pattern. Change your daily routine for a few days, read some type of book you have never read before, change the way you dress, grow a mustache, fix your hair in a new way, or invite people you do not know to your home. There are hundreds of ways to purposefully develop your flexibility without compromising your principles. Learn to experiment and take some risks. You will be a more mature and complete person as you learn to flow with change rather than fight it. Never allow your mind and will to petrify. Keep flexible.

Peaking Out

It was one of those meetings that management conducts periodically. It was the annual employee evaluation. Frequently, as they reviewed managers and supervisors, there would be comments like, "I'm afraid he's peaked out. No more promotions." or "She's reached the limit of her capacity " or "I think he's one step above his level of competency." or "He doesn't have the capacity for handling any more responsibility."

No one wants to "peak out" or "reach their limit." We may not want more responsibility, but we certainly resist the stigma of others knowing we have reached our limits. Yet limitations are part of life. No one is a superman. Not everyone can run a four-minute mile or type 110 words a minute. Only a few people can survive on four hours of sleep or work fourteen hours a day and still be refreshed. Some people thrive under pressure while others collapse. Some are master craftsmen while others can't even put together a Tinker Toy set with instructions. Life includes limitations and boundaries. Each person has distinct limitations as well as strengths.

One of the greatest steps to maturity occurs when we recognize and admit our limitations and live within them. This does not mean that we do not extend our limits and grow, but simply that we live realistically. The wise person knows when to say no and when to admit that he cannot do a particular task. Most pressure in mid-life, especially in work, stems from pushing our limits and living on the thin edge of our abilities. Such a lifestyle crushes us emotionally and physically.

One of the most freeing acts of life is discovering our personal limits and capabilities; then being satisfied with how God, in his sovereignty, made us.

We experience physical, mental, and emotional limitations all our lives. But these limits change with circumstances and age. Clearly we decline physically with age, but we should increase our mental and emotional limits. What may seem to be a decreased emotional capacity is often the result of an increase in emotionally draining circumstances.

Laziness and fear can cause us to accept limits that do

not actually exist. To avoid the risk of failure, or the pressure of stress, we often develop a "can't-do" philosophy of life. We become unwilling to exceed our imagined limits and become soft, lazy, and fearful. In mid-life the mature man or woman discerns the difference between real and imagined limits and acts accordingly.

In Romans 12:3 Paul warns us, "Don't cherish exaggerated ideas of yourself or your importance, but try to have a sane estimate of your capabilities by the light of the faith that God has given to you all" (PH). We are not to underestimate or overestimate our limits and abilities. Knowing our limits will free us to make an even greater contribution in the kingdom and will give peace of mind.

Paul also acknowledged God's sovereignty in his own background and abilities. "But by the grace of God I am what I am" (1 Corinthians 15:10). That's quite a statement—the admission of a middle-aged man at peace with both who he is and what he is doing in life. Paul could not alter his past as a persecutor of the church, but he could serve God to the limit in the future. That is the ideal mid-life attitude—acceptance of what is, optimism about the future, and a commitment to work to our limits.

So you're limited? So you've "peaked out?" What a blessing to know it, admit it, and live within your God-given bounds. What a tragedy to allow that discovery to send you into despair and self-recrimination. We must not be like the dog who beats a path around the edge of his fence, always testing and resenting his limits. Let's be like the gardener who beautifies the edges of his yard.

Financial Problems

Alan and Cindy are a rather typical middle-aged couple.

Alan has a good job. They have three children, two in college, a lovely home, two cars, and a recreation vehicle. They are both edgy and somewhat sharp with one another. They finally discuss their latest financial crisis with checkbook, bills, and budget in hand. They face a severe financial strain with no simple solutions. Revolving charge accounts total $3,000. Education loans total $9,000 to date with several years to go and one child still to enter college. Their house payment stretches their budget, and taxes went up again. They have reached the end of their resources.

Cindy is working part-time at a very low-paying job. She wonders if she should work full-time. They have stopped giving to their church. The last six months have been nothing short of miserable. She feels guilty every time she spends any money. Any question on Alan's part makes her angry. He is anxious about his situation at work, which makes their financial position even more critical. They are clearly overextended and cannot find a way out. They have become accustomed to moderate affluence and enjoy a measure of prestige among their friends. They fear losing their home. With Cindy working they need two cars. They finally decide that she should work full-time even though this will strain their relationship and curtail many of their Christian activities.

Does that sound familiar? Most of us relate only too well. Finances produce conflict at most stages of marriage, but in mid-life it is complicated by many other frustrations. The best cure is prevention, but that is empty advice for one already in financial straits. So let's examine a few of the major financial problems facing couples in mid-life.

Children in College

Each of us want the best for our children. So we do all we can to help them go to a college or trade school. We know the value of extra training and preparation. We sacrifice to help them as much as we can. This is good, but must be done within reasonable limits. Whether you have adequate resources or not, the children need to pay for some of the cost of their training. You may need to inform them of your financial situation and suggest they consider dropping out of school for a year to work.

The Problem of Materialism

Without question, ours is a materialistic society. We eat well, live in fine homes, and drive good cars. We long for luxuries and scrimp and save to get them. We even go into debt to acquire them. Why? Just because we want them. Frequently the Christian is no different from the non-Christian regarding his desire for material things. An unbiblical focus on comfort and ease should make us uncomfortable.

The problem comes when we lust for possessions and depend upon them for satisfaction. In fact, we put them so high on our priority list that we may overlook more critical financial needs later, not to mention the needs of the church and missions. Even when our attitude toward "things" is biblical (see Matthew 6:19-34), we may still be overextended financially through unwise purchases. After several years of financial struggle in our twenties, the purchase of a "dream house" often occurs in mid-life, adding extra financial pressure. Most of us tend to buy a home which taxes our income. We want it furnished immediately with our dream furniture.

We need to resist the materialistic tendencies thrust upon us by the non-Christian world. Jesus gave us some simple guidelines in Matthew 6:19-21.

Do not store up for yourselves treasures on earth,

> where moth and rust destroy, and where thieves break
> in and steal. But store up for yourselves treasures in
> heaven, where moth and rust do not destroy, and
> where thieves do not break in and steal. For where
> your treasure is, there your heart will be also.

Frequently, the financial strain of mid-life is caused by an accumulation of debts which all come due at the same time. It is one pressure which can be avoided by good planning and a scriptural view of sacrificial living.

Husband and Wife Both Working

The number of households where both husband and wife work in a secular job outside the home is increasing so rapidly that the concept of the "housewife" is fast becoming history. The pressures on the marriage and home are multiplied many times, especially since most husbands and children do not work around the house. They may still expect the wife to carry the load of housework. This creates a breeding ground for conflict at any stage of marriage.

With few exceptions, the major reasons for a wife working are related to finances. More money for the house, children in college, a nicer home, or an exciting vacation. Occasionally the wife simply wants to develop her own career or feels bored, but that is the exception.

What are some of the problems to be expected when both husband and wife work?

1. There will be more pressure and conflict over the normal functioning of the home.
2. The wife will be more tired and preoccupied.
3. There will be less time for ministry outreach and church involvement.
4. Time for the family will be limited.

5. Both partners will feel more financially independent and less dependent on each other.
6. The children can easily be neglected due to the parents' lack of time and energy.
7. The financial return may not be as high as you expect.[2]
8. In mid-life, this adds an extra emotional drain which will take its toll.

All of these things will not necessarily happen to you, but the potential is there. There are some good reasons for a wife to work. When all your children are in school or college, you may agree together to sacrifice by working to help pay for their education. Some women have a greater capacity and interests which are fulfilled significantly by a secular job. The main issues are that she must not neglect her primary responsibilities of family and husband. Carefully consider all the factors before launching out into the job market.

The inflated cost of buying a home is drawing more women to work. Many families simply cannot qualify for a loan on just the husband's salary. So they are forced to have two jobs to be able to buy a house. Again, we must ask, "Is it worth it?" When as a middle-aged couple, you decide the wife should work, carefully consider the additional, inevitable pressures.

In summary, we have found that finances are the number one cause of conflict and pressure in marriage. It matters little whether there is a lack of money or an abundance of it—conflict still occurs. In mid-life finances can be the focus for future security, or simply the means with which to live and serve God. Finances can be either a source of worry and anxiety, or a stimulus to faith. Finances can be a curse as you hoard and covet, or a blessing as you give and share. Even with increasing costs and needs in mid-life, we must return to the basic fact that God supplies all our needs. "And my God will meet all your needs according to his glorious riches in Christ Jesus" (Philippians 4:19).

Roots

George and Katherine Benton were alone. They went to parties, socialized, and invited people to dinner, but they had no close friends. Acquaintances, yes, but friends, no. Their roots were shallow and they longed for old friends, and the city they lived in previously. A job change transferred them four years ago, but their hearts never left. "No other church will ever be like that one. We can never afford the house we want here. People are so unfriendly in this city."

They frequently took trips back to their former city. Their phone bill grew like the national debt. They had been transplanted, but their roots were dying.

Because of our mobility, we rarely retain the same circles of friends for many years. Thus it is imperative that we be able to develop new friendships and roots. People in mid-life generally find it more difficult to develop new friendships and loyalties. For some reason we isolate ourselves and retreat at a time when we desperately need deep, understanding friendships. Most people make quality friendships in their twenties and early thirties. As life progresses, children come, a career demands more time, and people turn inward. In some ways this is natural as they find more fulfillment in their family and marriage. But as mid-life comes, and the family scatters, outside relationships become more important. Yet they are hard to develop. Age brings caution. The experiences of life make us more guarded. Pride and ego keep our friendships superficial. The lack of in-depth sharing on the spiritual level earlier in life now hinders us even more.

"A friend loves at all times, and a brother is born for adversity" (Proverbs 17:17). We need friends when we encounter trouble and difficulty. Yet we seldom develop friends in the midst of trouble. We may find sympathy, counsel, and concern, but rarely deep friendship. We must build such friendships earlier. We seldom see the need for friends until it is too late. We need both individual, personal friends, and friendships with couples. For a Christian, friendship must be based on a spiritual bond.

Close, rewarding friendships will not come naturally in mid-life. Therefore, we must seek them out aggressively. Like communication in marriage, friendship requires time and effort. Dinner once every three months and a "howdy" at church will not develop the relationship. It requires a combination of spiritual and social activities. As we seek friendship, we need common interests. We need to "click" in our relationships. The mature person learns to adapt to a wider variety of people. Pray that God will put you in touch with others who will become fast friends.

What about our "roots?" Roots are friendships and cause us to grow deeply into a community and a church. Begin working on new and deeper friendships. Don't withdraw into isolation in mid-life. As you extend yourself to others, you will find others need and appreciate your friendship too.

Recreation and Physical Health

"Do you not know that your body is the temple of the

Holy Spirit, who is in you, whom you have received from God? You are not your own; you were bought at a price. Therefore honor God with your body" (1 Corinthians 6:19-20). When we speak of protecting the body as God's temple we usually think of drugs, cigarettes, and alcohol. Certainly they are harmful for the body. But other factors do just as much harm. Overeating, a lack of proper nutrition, lack of sleep, carelessness in treating illness, overexertion, anxiety, and exhaustion all take their toll. They break down the body, make us miserable, and hinder productive functioning.

As we enter middle age, we are more sensitive to jokes about fat, potbellies, handles on the hips, shortness of breath, and a lack of energy. We fail to see the humor because these comments are all too true and frequently unnecessary. Most of us crash through the twenties with little concern for our physical and emotional needs, eating what we like, pushing our bodies to their limits, and caring little about exercise. Then we begin to gain weight, pull muscles, fall ill more easily, and lose energy—and we wonder why.

Certainly we do not have the brute strength we had at eighteen or twenty-five, but we can still have physical health and endurance. In fact, we can be stronger if we use our strength and energy more wisely. We tend to accept bulges and tiredness as a natural outcome of mid-life. But they are not natural. In fact, they are abnormal.

Dr. Hugh Pentney has stated this well. "If you compare a naked man of twenty-five—the age of peak physical perfection—with a normal man of forty-five, there need be very little external physical difference. If the older man has taken care of his body, he will almost certainly be as well-equipped to cope with every normal physical activity—apart from supreme feats of athleticism—as a man of twenty-five. And he can stay that way for years, for it is not our bodies that are faulty, but we who make them so. We do this through a combination of strain and abuse which is frequently the product of our own folly, both in the environment of our work and in our private lives."[3]

We are dying physically every day. Decay is part of living. But we hasten it by our careless lifestyles. The primary areas affecting us physically are:

- diet and nutrition
- exercise
- emotions and recreation

Before discussing these, we want to emphasize that none of them will naturally improve. They require decision and discipline—the same ingredients required for a godly life, a good marriage, success at work, and raising children. As you look at yourself in the mirror, or take your emotional temperature, what do you discover? Are you pleased with yourself? Are you happy with your physical condition? As an aid to further evaluation, respond to the following statements with a yes or no.

	Yes	No
I am within five pounds of my ideal weight.	____	____
I get regular exercise three times per week.	____	____
I eat a well balanced diet.	____	____
I am generally free of worry and anxiety.	____	____
I get adequate sleep.	____	____
I do have recreational activities.	____	____
I can walk a mile in eighteen minutes without being winded.	____	____

If you answered no more than twice you need to give some special attention to your physical condition.

Diet and Nutrition

In some Christian circles diet and nutrition have almost become a religion and eating unnatural or junk foods is almost considered a sin. Be careful about extremes in either diet or exercise and about your motives for dieting. Pride is not a good motive for losing weight. We should look healthy and trim but our appearance should be motivated by a desire to be an attractive witness for Christ rather than to attract attention to ourselves. We should also avoid crash diets, since they rarely keep the weight off and they put the body under extreme stress.

We urge you to limit the amount of food you eat. The best diet exercise is a push away from the table. Eat moderately and sensibly. In mid-life we neither need, nor can we use, the same quantity of food we ate in our teens and twenties. Only a few people are able to eat all they want and not gain weight. Even if you can, your trimness does not mean you are eating correctly. It simply means that weight gain is not a problem for you. Use a program that works for you—an agreement with a friend, a weight loss group, or a doctor checking on you. All diets require the common ingredient of discipline. Only you can supply it.

The subject of nutrition raises controversy whenever it is discussed. The Scriptures teach moderation and temperance in all things. We encourage a moderate, healthful lifestyle which gives you physical health, stamina, and energy. We can become so fussy with a diet that we offend some people. When traveling overseas and in our own country Mary and I have followed the principle, "Eat whatever is put before you without raising questions of conscience" (1 Corinthians 10:27). Here are some basic guidelines to build into your diet. Limit the intake of:

- fats and oils
- cholesterol and triglycerides
- sugar

As you adjust your eating habits, we suggest you examine two or three books on the subject and decide what areas of your current diet should change. It is wise to avoid fast food restaurants and instant meals.

Consult your physician before starting any radical diet. Make sure you have a blood test at least once every two years to check your levels of cholesterol and triglycerides.

You deserve a healthy body. A healthy body deserves, in fact demands, proper diet and nutrition. Once run down, the body is very difficult to rebuild. Begin protecting and preserving it now.

Exercise

Jogging, raquetball, and tennis have taken our country by storm. More people are aware of the need for physical exercise than ever before. Just as in the case of nutrition, jogging has raised considerable controversy. Whatever the precise analysis, no one questions the need and value of *regular* exercise which works the muscles, lungs, and cardiovascular system.

Most exercise will do you some good. The more balanced systems like Ken Cooper's *Aerobics* [4] develop the body in a gradual, controlled way with little danger of overexertion. Unless you are an extremely organized and disciplined person, you need something that is simple, easy to follow, and enjoyable. Begin a daily walking program of fifteen to thirty minutes. Don't think you will get enough from your normal day's activities. True, many women may walk a lot and climb many stairs, but generally that is not regular exercise. What you do must be done continuously for a period of time to build up your endurance.

What are some possibilities for exercise? Most authorities agree that swimming provides the most complete muscular and respiratory (cardiovascular) workout. However, not everyone swims well or has access to a pool.

The next most efficient exercise is jogging or running. Begin a program of walking/jogging gradually and with care. Start with as little as you need and work up to about one and a half to three miles. Remember that you need to exercise long enough so your body works hard. Anything under twenty minutes is of questionable value. If you run or jog don't neglect the most important piece of equipment you need—running shoes. They make the difference between enjoyment and drudgery, ease and injury. Invest in a good pair of shoes specifically designed for running. It will help you run better and protect your feet and legs from injury.

Other beneficial sports are:

- hiking
- bicycling
- climbing
- handball
- raquetball
- tennis
- basketball

Most men enjoy competitive sports more than straightforward exercise. They are often emotionally refreshing, which is as important as physical exercise. They can also provide opportunities for witnessing and fellowship.

In conjunction with jogging or other sports, a few minutes of calisthenics or stretching exercises should be included for warming up and preventing injury. In mid-life, we should not expect to play as hard or perform like we did at twenty-two.

If you *begin* exercising in mid-life, several suggestions are in order:

1. Get a physical. You should do this at least once every two years anyway.
2. Start a walking program *now*.
3. Start your exercise program slowly and gradually increase it. Do not crash into it as you would have in your twenties.
4. Include some exercise you really enjoy.
5. Resolve to keep going for at least two months. You need that long to get through the period of drudgery when you wonder if it's worth it.

You may think it is too late to start. It's never too late. We recently heard of a woman who began jogging in her sixties. She is now in her seventies and going strong. When asked if she had been sick, she replied, "Yes, I had the flu once for three hours!" Don't give in to the battle of the bulge. You have much to lose in the mid-years of your life and much to gain. Be a good steward of the body God has given you.

Emotions and Recreation

Emotions can damage your body as severely as can poor nutrition and lack of exercise. Happiness relates more to our emotions than to our physical beings. When we ask,

"How do you feel?" we rarely mean physical, but emotional well-being. Even though we discussed building emotional foundations in Chapter 6, we did not address how emotions affect physical well-being, both positively and negatively.

Dr. John Schindler, in his excellent book *How to Live 365 Days a Year* states, "Over 50% of all the illness that doctors see is emotionally induced illness!" He says further, "Occasionally a person can be objective enough to see that his life is a sea of troubles, but he usually remains unaware that he is having any such thing as emotional stress. Emotional stress is a pretty intangible sounding thing to most people and when their physical distress begins, they haven't the faintest idea that it is coming from their emotional stress."[5]

There are good emotions and bad emotions. Happiness and peace are clearly good, uplifting emotions. Anger and anxiety are examples of bad emotions. We can view emotions as incidents or patterns. We suggest you look at your pattern of emotional responses and strive for emotional stability and maturity. Good emotions heal and build us up, while bad emotions make us ill and destroy us. Thus we must guard and strengthen our emotional life as we do our bodies.

To this point we have discussed emotional foundations (Chapter 6), depression (Chapter 5) and other related emotional issues. Here we simply wish to highlight the need for positive control and development of our emotional being for the sake of our physical being.

Emotionally induced illness is *not* mental illness. But it is often initiated by emotional conflicts. Our emotions are intricately connected to our minds. Our emotions, which are normal functions of our mind/body system, warn us of the incidents of life about us.

We can do many things to control our emotions.

- Develop a close walk with God.
- Learn to handle anger.
- Learn to resolve conflict.
- Learn to cope with stress.
- Learn to trust God on a daily basis.
- Learn to pray.
- Develop our marriage relationship.

Although we believe the basic roots of emotional health lie in our daily relationship with God, nevertheless we often try to spiritualize things that have simple, practical solutions when combined with our walk with God.

One more key, practical issue can help our emotional development. Recreation. Not entertainment or amusement, but recreation. Recreation should *re-create* us mentally, emotionally, and physically. By studying the Latin root of the English word we learn that amusement means to "not think" (*a-not, muse-think*). Entertainment is usually *totally passive*. You can see why television rarely qualifies as recreation, for it is a passive form of entertainment and rarely stimulates our thinking. We all must have some type of recreation or we will suffer emotionally. We need a change of pace, something that refreshes. Recreation is not necessarily exercise, though exercise could be part of it. Recreation must be emotionally refreshing.

Recreation for one person can be pressure or drudgery to another. That highlights the problem of "family" recreation; what one family member enjoys, another may not. That is when compromise and helping another to enjoy an activity becomes important.

Some people particularly enjoy doing something alone: fishing, hiking, gardening, reading, hunting, bird-watching, sewing, knitting, performing or listening to music. Others like to do things with friends or the family: tennis, boating, skiing, work projects at home, car maintenance, camping, concerts, hobbies, arts and crafts, or decorating. The list can include dozens of other things. Some people enjoy long vacations or travel. Others just want to be with their family in some activity. When children are in their teens, much of your recreation involves attending their activities.

Try this short project. Write out a list of the kinds of activities you really *enjoy* doing—things that help *you* to relax. Leave two columns to the right. In the first column put how many days, weeks or months since you last did this. Then pick three or four items and put a date in the second column when you plan to do it again. Also put an asterisk (*) by each one that you would do with all or part of your family. For instance:

Play tennis.	16 months	next Thursday
*Go to a concert.	1 year	
*Take a two-day vacation.	4 months	within 2 months
*Go to a fair.	3 months	
*Have friends in our home.	3 weeks	in 1½ weeks
Read special books.	current	continue

If you have found, as we have, that several of these things have been neglected in the rush of daily living, it is a clue that we lack emotional rebuilding time. Also, if you had very few asterisks, you may need to develop some things to do with family or friends. If each activity had asterisks, you may need to learn the benefits of solitude by doing some things alone.

In some ways, recreation is an escape, but a very necessary and healthy escape. Learn to escape for the sake of your emotions. You will be paid back many times over with good health and peace of mind.

Certainly emotions can damage your health and make you ill. But the opposite is also true. Poor physical health deeply affects your emotions. One who is not in good physical condition is considerably more prone to emotional traumas. Physical conditioning and emotional building work together to preserve your total well-being.

Your body is the temple of the Holy Spirit. Don't abuse it. Build it up so you can accomplish your goals, and, more importantly, to serve God.

NOTES: 1. Eric Hoffer, "Points to Ponder," *Reader's Digest,* April, 1979, page 56.

2. George Fooshee, *You Can Be Financially Free* (Old Tappan, New Jersey: Fleming H. Revell Co., 1976), page 51.

3. Dr. Hugh Pentney, "Strip Jack Naked," *Royal Bank of Canada Monthly Letter,* October, 1979.

4. Kenneth H. Cooper, *The New Aerobics* (New York: Bantam Books, 1970).

5. John A. Schindler, M.D., *How to Live 365 Days a Year* (New York: Fawcett Publications #P2278, 1954), page XII.

CHAPTER 11

Ministry in Mid-life

Few people make their major contribution in life during their twenties or thirties. Mid life presents the most potentially productive and fulfilling era of life. Life to this point is preparation for this time. Yet many men and women allow the experiences of this time to so cripple them spiritually and emotionally that they give up and back away from a strong, vibrant contribution to society and the Body of Christ.

Jesus, like all Jewish men, did not begin his public ministry until he was thirty. Paul certainly was in his forties and fifties during his most fruitful ministry.

Is there any real advantage to middle age? What makes one more effective then as compared with other times of life? In this chapter we will not only examine the advantages, but also give specific suggestions on how to have a personal ministry in mid-life.

Advantages of Mid-life

Middle age is the time to fulfill the preparation of your

earlier years. "Most of the great achievements in history, in philosophy, statecraft, science and the arts, have been by people from the ages of forty to seventy." In a recent investigation of deceased artists, scientists, and scholars in sixteen fields of work, a British researcher found that "the most productive ages were from forty to fifty in almost all these groups. In only one field, chamber music, did the greatest productivity come earlier. Not until the age of sixty did the mathematicians included in the study hit their productive peak."[1] This brings us to the first advantage of mid-life.

Age
You may lament growing older, feeling the inevitable end of your life approaching. But an awareness of the brevity of life and your own fleeting years is very helpful. We must not resent time's passage, but welcome it. For in that realization comes the impetus for sharpening our priorities and concentrating on the important things in life.

Age brings respect. The apostle Paul listed respect as an initial qualification for the position of an elder (see Titus 1:6-9). Although the word *elder* in the New Testament does not refer only to age, it implies a certain maturity. Until a person is of a certain age, he should not carry certain positions of responsibility in the church.

A sense of authority also comes with age. Younger people more easily confide in you and ask for advice and help. Many of them do not feel comfortable talking with someone of their own age about certain problems or issues.

The world does not always honor age—not even middle age. Some younger people think that a person of fifty is "over the hill." The Christian community treats people differently than the world does. Christians view age with deference and respect.

Wisdom and Maturity

A person does not necessarily become wise and mature with age, although that should happen. As we grow older, we should develop into mature men and women who wisely apply the lessons of life. If you are truly maturing, your age will give you a splendid opportunity to minister to others. Wisdom comes from knowing and applying Scripture to your own life and then helping others apply it to their lives. The only true wisdom comes from God. "The fear of the Lord is the beginning of wisdom, and knowledge of the Holy One is understanding" (Proverbs 9:10).

One can be wise in the affairs of the world but foolish regarding spiritual things. No matter how astute one might be in business, true wisdom will not result without depth in the Scriptures. Similarly, maturity comes from the diligent application of God's word to erase immaturity and conform one to the image of Christ. Many sincere Christians do not mature and become wise because they have never allowed other wise men and women, or the Scriptures, to correct and instruct them. "Do not rebuke a mocker or he will hate you; rebuke a wise man and he will love you. Instruct a wise man and he will be wiser still; teach a righteous man and he will add to his learning" (Proverbs 9:8-9).

So, although wisdom and maturity can be yours, you must develop them.

Experience

Experience builds an irreplaceable bank of knowledge within every individual. In mid-life you can draw on your years of experience to share with others. But how can this resource be tapped and used? Many people have experience without understanding their past history. Experience without understanding can lead to a mid-life resentment crisis when you review your history and recognize that you did not learn from it. Every person has much to share, especially lessons learned from serious mistakes in early life. Real wisdom comes after seeing an error, correcting it, and showing others how to avoid it.

Your experience is a vast resource upon which you can draw to understand life, yourself, and others. Experience petrifies and hardens some people, developing prejudice and pigheadedness. Experience broadens others and makes them empathetic, wise, and understanding. When filtered through God's word and a godly life, experience becomes a master teacher and a valuable base for your ministry.

Growing Family

As your children grow up, you learn valuable lessons —many of them the hard way. You will make mistakes and learn from them. Younger people who know your expertise will naturally turn to you for advice and help with their families. This is a distinct advantage of mid-life. Think through what you have learned about raising a family so you can share those lessons with others, not as rules, but as principles for application.

Career Platform

Your work gives you a platform for a ministry to many people. Regardless of your job, certain people will respect you and listen to you for what you do. A coal miner may not listen to an accountant, but he will listen to a mechanic or factory worker. A pharmacist may not listen to a truck driver but he will listen to a doctor or engineer. Each career is valuable and has its particular audience. God has placed you in your job and career to give you a context from which you can speak and testify.

In mid-life your career is developing to its fullest. Often you are most at ease with your abilities, even You are changing jobs. You know what you can and can't do. By mid-life you should have confidence in your direction, and be stable and productive. This is your best time for an outreach and ministry.

Developing Your Ministry

Ministry. Isn't that what ministers do? Isn't it just the paid clergy who have a ministry? Absolutely not.

Ministry is a word which describes something every Christian should do. The word *minister* comes from a Latin word meaning "servant." A ministry is serving others with the gifts and abilities God gave you.

Should a ministry be a full-time occupation?

No. A full-time ministry should be the exception rather than the rule.

Most ministry is done by the laity—men and women who live and work in the world. Ideally, a full-time pastor or worker is a specialist and a facilitator who helps the laity do *their* ministry.

So what exactly is a ministry? A ministry is a specific task in the Body of Christ to which you are called. It could be teaching Sunday school, evangelism, serving, or any number of other functions in the church.

To put your ministry in perspective with the rest of your life, refer back to Figure 4-1 on page 92. You can have a ministry only when Christ, family, and job are balanced. Your ministry should flow out of your life. First your life must be centered in Christ and you must be growing as his disciple. This will include a daily devotional life, prayer, regular study of the Scriptures, and submitting to his lordship.[2] Second, if your family life is not in order, you have no home base from which to minister. Third, you need to maintain a witness in your job by how you work.

Definition of Ministry

Now let's be specific on types and definitions of ministry. There are two basic types of ministry.

1. Outreach ministry. This reaching out to non-Christians to help them come to know Christ. It can include direct witnessing as well as serving and helping others.
2. Ministry to the Body of Christ. This is a ministry to those who are already Christians. This type of ministry breaks down into two categories:
   Discipling, which includes the follow-up of new Christians and helping them grow to maturity.
   Caring for (or shepherding) those in the Body who have special needs (the elderly, the sick, and those who need counseling, for example).

Every Christian should do some ministry of both types—evangelism and ministry to the Body. But how? What practical things can we do in these two areas?

Outreach

The foundation for outreach to the lost is a firm conviction that we have a direct commission from God to reach the world for Christ. "But you will receive power when the Holy Spirit comes on you; and *you will be my witnesses* in Jerusalem, and in all Judea and Samaria, and to the ends of the earth" (Acts 1:8). We have no option. We must witness to those who don't know Christ. But we need to learn how. Witnessing involves more than giving out tracts or bringing people to a gospel meeting at church. We need to know other ways to reach out.

Conduct an investigative Bible study. This is a study in your home with non-Christians who agree to study a portion of the Bible for four to six weeks. We've used the Gospel of John.[3]

Conduct a women's evangelistic tea or coffee. Simply invite primarily non-Christian women to your home for tea or coffee and to hear a brief presentation by another woman. This would usually be a testimony or stimulating discussion of an interesting topic related to the gospel. Later you could organize a home Bible study or meet with some of the women individually to share the gospel in more detail.

Host an Andrew dinner or dessert. After Andrew met Christ, he immediately brought his brother, Peter, to Christ. Christians bring non-Christians to an "Andrew" dinner. This evangelistic event works well with both couples and singles. The idea is similar to the evangelistic tea, since you have dinner or dessert followed by a speaker and discussion. Always inform your guests that a discussion on Christianity will be included so they are not surprised when it occurs.

Have people in your home. Use your home as a point of outreach. Invite people in for dinner, to watch a football game on television, for dessert, or for games. Befriend them and let them see what a Christian home is like. Look for natural opportunities for sharing your faith.

Neighborhood evangelism. Begin praying for your neighbors. Invite them in socially at various times. Organize a neighborhood Bible study with women, men, or couples.

Problem counseling with non-Christians. Keep alert for those at work or in your neighborhood who are hurting and in need. Marriage problems, difficulties with teens, or physical illness can all provide opportunities to serve and help. Through helping them you may have the opportunity to share Christ as you demonstrate his love.

Calling on church contacts. Visitors to church make a natural set of contacts for evangelism. Programs like Evangelism Explosion use a church visitation program to secure opportunities for presenting the gospel.

Children's evangelism. Children are fertile ground for the gospel. Most people make their commitment for Christ when they are children or teens. Child Evangelism Fellowship and similar organizations are good vehicles for reaching children in the community. Through children you may also reach their parents.

Youth outreach. Some people relate well to teens and should put their efforts into an outreach to them. Church youth groups, and organizations like Youth for Christ and Young Life have opportunities for adults to serve by helping to reach teenagers.

All of these are fine ideas. But ideas do not work by themselves. The key is to *do something*, not just talk or think about it. Often we are reluctant to evangelize because we do not know how to share the plan of salvation. Learn how to do this from your pastor, or friends, so you can clearly share the gospel.

Ministry to Believers

A ministry to the Body of Christ is just as necessary. Not everyone can preach or be a great leader. But there are many vital opportunities and essential services that most people can fill behind the scenes. Here are some suggestions:

Teaching. Sunday schools are usually short of good teachers for adults, young people, and children. If you do teach, become involved in the lives of your students. Give your time to the children in social events, outings, and personal contact. They need interaction with adults to help them come to know Christ and to grow and mature.

Club programs. Christian Service Brigade and Pioneer Girls, as well as other church youth programs, provide opportunities for adults to develop in-depth relationships with children other than on Sunday mornings. Dedicated leaders are greatly needed to work with young people and children in the context of crafts, outdoor events, and practical skills. Children respond to down-to-earth contacts. Many non-Christian children who attend these programs can be reached for Christ.

Church offices. The task of an elder or deacon is one of the most important in the church. Elders do not simply meet for church business. Rather they provide a significant ministry to people.

Music. Many people enjoy music and can participate in the choir or other music programs. Children's choirs provide a valuable service by helping children learn to love music and to worship through music.

Home Bible studies for Christians. One of the most rewarding contexts for fellowship in the church is a small group studying the word on a regular basis. You can either lead, be a participant, or simply open your home. This is one of the few places where you get involved in personal investigation of Scripture. Also, you develop deep relationships with others in the study.

Planning. Every church needs people who plan the activities and direction of the fellowship. The pastor cannot do it all. Committees and short-term planning teams will always need people who are eager to serve and help. Much of this effort involves behind the scenes hard work which someone must do. These people are special load-lifters for the pastor and the entire congregation. The idea for an event is just the beginning. The detailed execution requires ninety percent of the work.

Hospitality. Some people minister through hospitality. They open their homes, invite people in, and make them feel welcome. This is far more than simple entertainment. It involves extending yourself when it may not be convenient as well as when you plan for it. Hospitality is a special gift. It includes bringing others, both Christian and non-Christian, into your home and family and extending yourself beyond your normal social obligations.

Person-to-person discipling. Learn to help another person grow to maturity in Christ. Seldom does one grow to his full capacity as a natural by-product of simply attending church. Much spiritual learning is communicated on a person-to-person basis. In this intimate way people open their lives and share real needs.[4]

Person-to-person counseling. Counseling presents one of the most demanding burdens in a pastor's work. Usually, by the time he is consulted, a problem is quite serious. Many people can learn to counsel effectively in problem situations. If you find yourself frequently listening to others' problems, you may be one with whom people share easily. This gives you the opportunity to help *if* you are qualified through experience or training and know what to do. Think of the load this would lift for the pastoral staff of your church. A key is getting some training as well as knowing the limits of your counseling ability.

Youth ministry. Every church needs people who can work effectively with the youth. It is a task with special demands. You must relate to them on a personal basis, open your home to them, and be available at odd hours. Teenagers need both couples and singles who will be their adult confidants and counselors.

Serving. Many tasks in the Body involve simply serving—doing things behind the scenes to make activities easier for others. Mailings, secretarial work, finances, janitorial work, printing, and building repairs must be done. But they do not get done without someone taking responsibility. If you are gifted in one of these areas, you can make a significant personal contribution by serving.

Administration. This is closely related to serving. Administrators can handle many business items and help a church function properly. Building scheduling, transportation, and budgeting are only a few of the many tasks in this type of ministry.

Missions. A church without a missions program is like a body without a soul—empty and focused only on itself. But a concern for missions does not just materialize. It takes concerned people who plan how to make others more aware of world needs and who can motivate people to pray and give. Each church should keep in touch with the missionaries it supports, know their needs and current concerns. Churches don't write letters, people do. You could have a ministry by writing to your church's missionaries.

Identifying and Implementing Your Ministry

Knowing what can be done as a ministry is still a far cry from doing it. Knowledge is ten percent. Action is ninety percent. Even though one is mentally convinced that a personal ministry is essential for a growing Christian, identifying a sphere of service and starting is often difficult. First, consider what every Christian should do.

The Standard for All Christians
No one can do everything, but everyone can do

something. Certain fundamental activities must be part of every Christian's life if they are to be happy, balanced, and fulfilled in their personal ministry.

1. Every Christian should do some kind of evangelism or outreach. When we minister only to those in the Body of Christ we turn inward and lose our vision for the lost.

2. Every Christian should develop one major ministry involvement of either the outreach or Body ministry type. This one ministry is what you concentrate upon and give yourself to. All others become subservient to it. Too many people try to do too many things and so do none of them well. Concentrate solidly upon a few strategic activities.

3. Every Christian should be discipled or helped by another more mature Christian. We all need accountability and training. Seldom does one develop in a healthy way totally alone. We need a mentor, not to control us, but to train and build us up in the faith.

4. Every Christian should be discipling another. The essence of life is physical and spiritual reproduction. We must not only aid in the birth of new Christians, but we must also help them grow and mature. This need not mean that your major ministry is discipling, but it is a part of your ministry. A parent's first responsibility is discipling his own children. Our churches are filled with people who desperately need help with their spiritual growth. But few Christians are willing to help or know how to help.

The underlying prerequisites for any ministry are our personal walk with God and a deep love for others. Without these elements you will not have a ministry—only activities and schedules. Without a deep walk with God your ministry may appear religious, but will actually be hollow and empty. Don't neglect your own spiritual life.

How To Select Your Ministry

Make a copy of the chart in Figure 11-1. The first task is to review the kinds of ministry listed in this chapter. Add other ministries that you think of. Put a check in the first column for those you are currently involved in.

Next, put a check in the second column for those ministries you have done in the past.

Review the list again and put a check in the third column by those ministries you feel you could do with proper training. Include those which you have already done or are already doing.

MINISTRY INTEREST AND ABILITY SURVEY

	Already Doing	Have Done Before	Could Do	Would Like To Try
OUTREACH				
MINISTRY TO BELIEVERS				

Figure 11-1

Finally, select three or four activities from each section which you would like to try if you had the opportunity. Put a check by these activities in the fourth column. You can include ones you are already doing if you want to keep doing them.

You have now completed a rough interest and ability survey for your potential ministry. You can use this chart in several ways. It will form the basis of a later activity— actually selecting your ministry. See how many checks in the last column match up with checks in the first column. The more they match, the better. The fewer matches or correlations the more likely you will want to alter your activity schedule.

Now to actually plan your ministry. Refer to Figure 11-2 on page 265. Before you can plan, you need to evaluate where you stand now. These questions will help you identify your personal needs.

Figure 11-3 (page 266) will help you plan for your ministry. The personal growth section helps you discover if you need to prepare before launching into your ministry. From Figure 11-1 select two or three items under "Would-Like-to-Try." Then make a specific plan for each of them. You need not do them all at once, but can stagger them over several weeks.

As you evaluate yourself and try to determine your best ministry, discuss it with your spouse, family, pastor, and a close Christian friend. They can give you good insight into yourself. Then try one of the ministries on a small scale for a few weeks or months. For instance, you might substitute as a teacher or observe a class for a while. After you have tried it, evaluate your performance. Then you could try another ministry for a short time.

Determine what further training or instruction you need to do a particular ministry. If you need to develop

PLANNING MY MINISTRY
CURRENT SITUATION

1. What ministries/activities am I currently involved in?

   _____

   _____

   _____

2. Considering the four "musts" for a Christian,

   What evangelism am I doing? _____

   What is my *major* ministry? _____

   Who is helping me grow? _____

   Who am I discipling? _____

3. Of the ministries listed in item 1, which coincide with the "Would-Like-to-Try" column of the ministry survey?

   _____

   _____

4. Do I believe that I am now doing my *major* ministry?

   Yes ____ No ____

5. If not, do I have time to add another ministry activity without canceling something else?

   Yes ____ No ____

6. If I cannot add another ministry activity, what current activity could I delete? _____

   _____

Figure 11-2

PLANNING MY MINISTRY
FOR THE FUTURE

PERSONAL GROWTH	Satisfactory	Need to Do What I Know	Need Further Help
Daily Devotions			
Personal Bible Study			
Prayer			
Witnessing			

MINISTRY	Can Do It Now	Must Get Training	Training Available
1.			
2.			
3.			

Figure 11-3

SPECIFIC PLAN FOR
MY MINISTRY

Specific plan for _____
(name the ministry)

Date to accomplish

1. Investigate opportunities. _____

2. Find out how to get
   training. _____

3. Get training. _____

4. Begin this ministry. _____

Specific plan for _____
(name the ministry)

1. Investigate opportunities. _____

2. Find out how to get
   training. _____

3. Get training. _____

4. Begin this ministry. _____

Specific plan for _____
(name the ministry)

1. Investigate opportunities. _____

2. Find out how to get
   training. _____

3. Get training. _____

4. Begin this ministry. _____

Figure 11-4

some special skills such as counseling, leadership, or leading Bible studies, don't delay learning those skills. Finally, plan on entering your ministry fully within one year. Figure 11-4 (page 267) may help you set some specific goals.

How to Have a Ministry in Mid-life

Effectively doing a ministry is not always an easy task. Many hindrances crop up to sidetrack or derail you. Here are a few suggestions.

Be as Mature as You Look

"Reaching the mental state of middle age is an achievement which some people never enjoy; there is something desperately forlorn about a person in his forties or fifties who still has a juvenile mentality."[5] When people reach mid-life, they can dress well and have an air of maturity. But when they speak, you realize they are pitifully immature as Christians. They simply have not grown up spiritually. And, in many cases, they have not grown up emotionally. The mid-life person frantically trying to look youthful reveals his immaturity. Your mid-life effectiveness will be in direct proportion to your mid-life maturity. But how do you achieve maturity? We cannot repeat our past to acquire maturity. But we can mature now. Here are some practical suggestions:

1. Accept your age and abilities. Do not pretend to be younger than you are or something that you are not.
2. Admit your personal spiritual need for growth.
3. Begin regular *study* of the Scriptures so you have a base from which to share.

4. Develop a serious, spiritual view of life. Guard against frivolous talk and actions. Humor and laughter are good, but guard against meaningless talking, jesting, and gossip.
5. Spend time with people who are mature and spiritual.
6. Guard against being opinionated on trivial issues.
7. Ask your spouse to help you with your appearance and public conduct.
8. Develop personal physical and spiritual discipline.
9. Read and do things that develop your mind.

We must grow up physically, mentally, socially, and spiritually. Luke 2:52 describes Jesus' development. "And Jesus grew in wisdom and stature, and in favor with God and men." This does not mean that every person must be suave, urbane, and dignified. You must be yourself, but make sure you have personal spiritual depth in your life. Your ministry should grow out of your spiritual maturity.

Develop Stability

A mark of maturity is stability in spiritual matters and life in general. In mid-life many destabilizing factors come into our lives. One of our greatest tasks is to remain stable through various storms and trials. "Therefore, my dear brothers, stand firm. Let nothing move you. Always give yourselves fully to the Lord because you know that your labor in the Lord is not in vain (1 Corinthians 15:58).

Keep Your Work Demands in Balance

Many men panic and try to make a final drive for success in their career. This pressure can prevent them from developing their spiritual ministry. Most gifted people are frequently so consumed by their work that they have little time for their families, much less a ministry.

Phillip Rand knew what God wanted him to do. He knew he needed to grow spiritually and give more time to a personal ministry and to his family. Yet he wanted to succeed in his career so badly that he consumed ten to fourteen hours a day at work. He acknowledged his need to work less, but his inner compulsion would not let him. Year after year he planned for a more relaxed work schedule. Yet he never accomplished his goal. A successful businessman, Phillip resigned himself to being an undeveloped, immature Christian. He had no depth and no personal ministry. Later in life he sensed his own emptiness, but could not break out of his ever-increasing cycle of work. Pride now kept him from becoming a learner. He held responsible positions in the church, but inwardly he knew he lacked spiritual depth. Finally he could live the masquerade no longer and withdrew to a meager habit of perfunctory church attendance.

What a sad mistake! What a loss to the Body of Christ! "But seek first his kingdom and his righteousness, and all these things will be given to you as well" (Matthew 6:33). God can make you successful without being consumed and controlled by your work. Delaying your spiritual growth until later rarely works. Act now, while the Holy Spirit is speaking to you about it.

Don't Procrastinate

The temptation to delay entering a personal ministry until later lures us into inaction. We panic and do the most pressing things while ignoring the most crucial. Once we understand our need to develop a ministry, we must not delay, or we will lose our conviction.

If you are forty or forty-five now it may take five years to fully develop a fruitful ministry. A depth of ministry does not come in a matter of months, but in years.

If you wait until you are fifty-five, you will lose ten years and will be far less likely to ever begin. The older you get, the harder it is to start something new. There will certainly be exceptions for those who are particularly teachable and determined in later life. One man we know closed his business at age fifty-seven to follow his deep conviction that God wanted him in a full-time ministry. He moved 1,000 miles to get the training he needed. He had become a Christian in mid-life and strongly pursued spiritual growth and maturity.

Procrastination is deadly. It wastes many years of potential growth and fruitfulness. Don't allow time to slip away as you consider beginning your personal ministry.

Mid-life can be your greatest time of productivity and fulfillment. There are so many significant advantages in age and experience. Yet many men and women begin giving up and thinking they are "over the hill." In reality, they are just reaching the right age and maturity for fulfilling a significant role in the church.

You can have a significant ministry. But only you can start your ministry. When will you begin?

NOTES: 1. "Who's Afraid of Middle Age?" *Royal Bank of Canada Monthly Letter,* October, 1979, page 2.

2. Walt Henrichsen, *Disciples are Made, Not Born* (Wheaton, Illinois: Scripture Press, Victor Books, 1974).

3. A good reference for leaders is *Leader's Guide for Evangelistic Bible Studies* (Colorado Springs, Colorado: NavPress, 1973). For use in a small non-Christian group, try *God, Man, and Jesus Christ* (Colorado Springs, Colorado: NavPress, 1978).

4. To help another Christian grow, read LeRoy Eims' book *The Lost Art of Disciplemaking* (Colorado Springs,

Colorado: NavPress, 1978). Also refer to Francis Cosgrove's book *Essentials of New Life* (Colorado Springs, Colorado: NavPress, 1979).

5. "Who's Afraid of Middle Age?" *Royal Bank of Canada Monthly Letter,* October, 1979, page 2.

CHAPTER 12

New Vistas—
An Exciting Future

One man in mid-life looks back, looks at himself, grumbles, becomes fearful, and withdraws, never wanting to face the reality of life again. He has begun to die.

Another man in his mid years, looks back, looks at himself, then looks to God and the future, and launches out with the mental fervor of his youth and lives his life to the fullest. He has been rejuvenated.

The difference between them is found in their view of the essence of life. For one man life means his future, not his past. His life is planted in a belief in the sovereign control of God. With this view, the future is as bright as the promises of God. Life is based on hope, not regret.

A positive mental and spiritual attitude brings every event into perspective through the light supplied by God's word. In this concluding chapter we want to set the stage for your personal action in the years ahead.

Perspective on Life

We each develop a perspective on life as we grow older. We

develop attitudes and ideas that color our entire view of life. Several factors can help us develop a positive, dynamic attitude toward our personal future.

Time

> Time is the most undefinable yet paradoxical of things; the past is gone, the future has not come, and the present becomes the past even while we attempt to define it, and, like the flash of the lightning, at once exists and expires.[1]

Time is our most precious commodity. But none of us knows how much of it we possess. If, in mid-life, we lament over the time that is gone, we will never learn to live in the present and prepare for the future. We learn from the past. We do not live in the past.

Time and age are inextricably related. Often, when we think of time we relate it to our age. We tend to think of how little rather than how much time we have. A life perspective which focuses on the present and the future provides a better view of life. We recount the blessings of God in the past, but we experience the blessings of God today. The past supplies wisdom and strength for today and tomorrow, but offers no means of changing our history.

God clearly teaches his perspective on time. "For a thousand years in your sight are like a day that has just gone by, or like a watch in the night" (Psalm 90:4). Time is not the crucial issue for God. What counts with him is character. He is interested in the person as well as what they do. God wants us to be aware that time is transient. The psalmist prayed, "Show me, O Lord, my life's end and the number of my days; let me know how fleeting is my life. You have made my days a mere handbreadth; the span of my years is as nothing before you. Each man's life is but a breath" (Psalm 39:4-5). In view of life's brevity we pray, "Teach us to number our days aright, that we may gain a heart of wisdom" (Psalm 90:12).

An awareness of time causes us to concentrate on serving God with the best of our lives. God wants us to live the years we have left to the maximum. He desires a full commitment to serving him with both time and energy. Thus, when we view our time as God's time, we become stewards who spend it only as he directs. But we tend to focus so much on ourselves, our own comfort, desires, and plans that we drown God's will in a flood of self-satisfaction. Such a perspective leads only to regret and despair. Realizing the futility of doing anything else rather than serving God gives a new hope and purpose to the future.

If God has granted us the privilege of living to mid-life, we have a unique set of experiences upon which we can build for the future. So our future is bright. With the maturity of age and experience, we can minister to others on the basis of what God has done in our lives. Thankfulness and anticipation should mark our perspective at this turning point in life. Let's live today to the fullest by serving God, and putting the past and the future into God's perspective on life.

Blaise Pascal, the French mathematician, wrote,

> Let any man examine his thoughts, and he will find them ever occupied with the past or the future. We scarcely think at all of the present; or if we do, it is only to borrow the light which it gives for regulating the future. The present is never our object; the past and the present we use as means; the future only is our end. Thus, we never live, we only hope to live.[2]

Being a Learner

Cato, the Roman scholar, started studying Greek when he was over eighty. Someone asked why he tackled such a difficult task then. "It's the earliest age I have left," said Cato, and went right on studying. When a person stops learning, he begins dying. Sadly, only rarely does he realize that he is dying. The secret of finding happiness and fulfillment in mid-life, apart from direct spiritual renewal, is being a learner. The one who constantly seeks to learn and develop will never dry up emotionally or mentally.

The author of Proverbs wrote, "Let the wise listen and add to their learning, and let the discerning get guidance" (Proverbs 1:5). On the other hand, "Fools despise wisdom and instruction" (Proverbs 1:7).

A hallmark of youth is the desire and ability to learn. But something strange happens as we grow older. We should know many things, but we feel we do not. We should be wise, but we may not be. Then pride keeps us from revealing our need and we close our minds to new ideas and teaching. When we lose our ability or our desire to learn, we seal our fate and shrivel and fade in mid-life. But if we continue to develop and expand our knowledge, experience, and abilities, we will keep growing. For the person who remains a learner, there is no limit to the potential of life in the midyears.

Thus, being a learner gives a positive, rejuvenating perspective on life which will sustain us through any adversity in mid-life.

Learning to Live with Stress

Stress is a reality of life. It always has been. All that changes over the years is the growing respect and appreciation for the effects of stress. In a Harvard study on aging, the one common contributor to good physical and emotional health was reported to be the ability to respond well to stress.* The adverse consequences of stress are ulcers, heart trouble, high blood pressure, depression, and many other physical and emotional illnesses.

A healthy perspective on life views stress as normal, but temporary. In fact, it is not the stress itself which causes the problems, but our emotional response to it. Each personality type tends to respond differently to various stresses. Some fight. Others worry and fret. Others become angry. Some withdraw or quit. A few press on as though the stresses did not exist.

Regardless of how mature and spiritual we may be, we will all respond initially to stress according to our personality and background. The key is what follows the initial response. If we continue to react negatively, we will suffer. But if we are alert to stress and respond biblically, we can avoid its negative effects.

"Do not be anxious about anything, but in everything, by prayer and petition with thanksgiving, present your requests to God. And the peace of God, which transcends all understanding, will guard your hearts and your minds in Christ Jesus" (Philippians 4:6-7). This is one of the most practical promises in Scripture for our emotional peace of mind. Applying it is not as easy as quoting it, however. The promise is rooted in the sovereignty of God. If you learn to live with stress, you will greatly enhance your enjoyment and fulfillment in mid-life.

Your Plan for the Future

The great manufacturer Charles Kettering said, "My interest is in the future because I am going to spend the rest of my life there."[3] The future comes whether we want it to or not. Will we welcome it with a ready plan and purpose, or fight it, resenting its intrusion with fear and trepidation? The Christian in mid-life owns every resource for making the future the happiest time of his or her life. God promises us power to live. "His divine power has given us *everything* we need for life and godliness through our knowledge of him who called us by his own glory and goodness" (2 Peter 1:3).

All of our personal life experiences have prepared us for a future under God's direction. Without God's direction and control, we will have very little hope or encouragement. Without his control our lives are rootless and shifting. If we live under his control, we have an eternal point of reference and direction.

Now is the time for some self-evaluation. To make a plan for your future, you need to know where you are *now*. Self-evaluation is not always easy, for we are frequently blind to our own needs. Evaluate yourself with the help of your spouse or a close friend. Briefly review each of the previous chapters and make some extra notes on your key personal needs. Even though you may not be experiencing any kind of mid-life crisis, there still is a need for evaluation and planning for the future.

Consider the charts in Figures 12-1 and 12-2, which are on pages 281 and 282. Make a copy of these to fill out, or use the ones in this book. The purpose of the chart in Figure 12-1 is to help you identify issues you are experiencing now. Figure 12-2 will help you determine an overall picture of both your past and present. After completing these evaluations choose several areas in which you would like to develop. Then select one or two of these areas to begin developing first. Refer to the suggestions in the earlier chapters for specifics in various areas which you are concerned about

The keys to making any kind of change effectively are:

1. Recognize and admit your need.
2. Carefully define your need.
3. Make a decision to take positive steps to meet the need.
4. Begin a plan of action, *now.*

Use the format in Figure 12-3 (page 283) for your personal development plan. For example:

Description of need: We have been communicating less and less as husband and wife. We have noticed increasing irritability and conflict. We are so busy at church, on the job, and with our teens that we don't have enough time together.

Ideas on how to meet the need: Talk daily. Go to dinner alone once a week. Get a weekend away. Set aside one night a week to be together. Drop one activity. No overtime for one month. Read a book together on communication.

Specific Plans	**Start By** (date)	**Complete By**
1. Go to dinner to discuss a plan to improve communication.	Next weekend	Same
2. Set aside at least five minutes per day for talking privately.	Next Monday	Try for two weeks
3. Read *Getting to Know You.*	Nov. 5	Dec. 5
4. Get two days away together.	Set date by Nov. 15	Jan. 15

Another example:

Description of need: I have been very tired and down emotionally. I know I am overweight and eating poorly. I think at least part of my problem is poor nutrition and a lack of exercise.

Ideas on how to meet the need: Have a physical examination. Start an exercise program. Improve my eating habits. Start jogging. Develop better sleep habits.

Specific Plans	Start By (date)	Complete By
1. Begin walking one mile each day for five of seven days a week.	Tomorrow/ Feb. 16	Continue
2. Get a physical check-up.	Mar. 1	Same
3. Begin my jogging program.	Day after Physical Exam	Continue 4 times per week
4. Stop snacking.	Now	Continue
5. Reduce the amount of food I eat (by one moderate helping), and by cutting sweets and starches out of my diet	Begin now and taper off in two weeks to a reduced amount.	Check progress each month.

We want to emphasize that if you do not make a plan (it doesn't *have* to be written), you very likely will not do anything about your need. Wishful thinking should never substitute for action.

Along with the areas you identified for yourself, we

IDENTIFYING CURRENT ISSUES

1. List some of the indications of mid-life which you have experienced to this point.

   _____

   _____

   _____

   _____

   _____

   _____

2. List one or two areas of your life that are of the greatest concern to you now.

   _____

   _____

   _____

3. What problem areas do you feel you have resolved to your satisfaction?

   _____

   _____

   _____

4. What one area is crucial to begin work on immediately?

   _____

   _____

   _____

Figure 12-1

EVALUATION

ISSUES	Stable	Has Been or Is a Crisis	Changing	Needs Change
Marriage				
—Communication				
—Physical Relationship				
Children				
—Teenagers				
—Tagalongs				
—Grandchildren				
Career				
Success				
Depression				
Singleness				
Ministry				
Physical Health				
Physical Appearance				
Spiritual Foundations				
Spiritual Maturity				
Flexibility				
Finances				

Figure 12-2

DEVELOPMENT PLAN

Description of Need: _____

_____

_____

_____

Ideas on How to Meet the Need: _____

_____

_____

_____

_____

_____

_____

Specific Plans	Start By (date)	Complete By
1. _____	_____	_____
_____		
2. _____	_____	_____
_____		
3. _____	_____	_____
_____		
4. _____	_____	_____
_____		

Figure 12-3

suggest that you set some goals in the following areas.

Examine your *personal relationship with God* to see if you are becoming a spiritually mature person. The joy and freedom of maturity gives a confidence and satisfaction that nothing else can give. Pick some particular area of your spiritual life to develop and improve.

Next, look at your *marriage relationship*. Mid-life is the turning point for many aspects of your life together. Patterns and problems which are not changed or corrected now will probably not change later. The very incidents which occur in the midyears disturb and cultivate the ground so that new qualities can grow and develop in your marriage.

Finally, remember that your life is not complete without some ministry to others. God does not want any of us to live only for ourselves. Even when we are doing well spiritually, have an excellent marriage, and good family relationships, the absence of a personal ministry to others severely dulls the enjoyment that could exist.

One of the most encouraging and emotionally uplifting activities of mid-life is personal development and education. At a time when life often stagnates, new inputs will stimulate and encourage us. Whether the development relates to job or personal life matters little. What counts is an aggressive, constructive development. Often both men and women in mid-life seek personal growth through further education. Correspondence courses, night classes, craft schools, and reading can all be part of your learning plan. Part of being a learner is to keep exploring. Seek out positive new experiences. Do things you have never tried before. Learn new subjects, skills, and activities individually, as a couple and as a family.

We took a short Greek course together. Jerry took ski lessons with Steve. Mary began learning violin with Kris. Other couples learn tennis together or read books and discuss them. Some build a new addition onto their house.

Never stop learning, developing, and growing.

As part of your plan for the future, develop relationships with younger people. Most of us minister downward in age. As a couple, you can have significant relationships with younger couples. Of course, you aren't going through the same things they are, but you did once, and it was not so very long ago. Many young couples would welcome a sincere friendship with an older couple. You may wonder how you can do this since you move in different social circles. Here are some ideas:

1. Initiate the relationships by inviting young couples to your home or to some event.
2. Use your children as a point of contact. Your youngest may be around the age of a younger couple's oldest child.
3. When asked for advice and counsel, do all you can to give helpful, practical advice and suggestions.
4. Find mutual interests and activities which you could do together.
5. Don't expect an exclusive relationship with younger couples, since they will also have peer relationships.
6. Don't try to dress and act young or chic. Dress and act your age and let your maturity attract them.
7. Do some Bible study with younger couples or in separate men's or women's groups.
8. Extend your friendship, help, and concern unselfishly and you will find relationships developing naturally.

We greatly value our friendship and interests with those our own age. But we would be far poorer if we did not have a number of close friendships with younger singles and couples. They need our maturity and experience. We need their youthful challenge and stimulation.

The Best Part of Life

The title of Ray Ortlund's fine book on mid-life, *The Best Half of Life* summarizes what we feel. Mid-life is the best part of life![4]

One of the most challenging parts of mid-life is that you can now be part of the backbone of your church. In many cases you are already regarded as the church's backbone whether you want to be or not. People naturally look to men and women who show maturity. You can provide some of the leadership and direction needed in your congregation.

If you do not give leadership, who will? Your role may not be "out-front" in a place of public leadership, but your contribution will be just as vital through behind-the-scenes work and service. Both public and private ministries need the maturity of your years and experiences. But above all, both require spiritual maturity to qualify for the position.

To this point in your life others have invested in you. Now you can invest your life in others. The return on your investment will be personal fulfillment and growth.

Though many of the younger set would fail to understand, few, if any, middle-aged people would choose to return to their twenties. What they have lost in youth they gain in wisdom and maturity. Only one thing can keep mid-life from being best for you—your attitude toward it and what you do with it.

NOTES: 1. Charles Caleb Colton, in *The International Encyclopedia of Thoughts* (Chicago: J. G. Ferguson Publishing Company, 1969), page 723.
2. Blaise Pascal, in *The International Encyclopedia of Thoughts,* page 581.
3. Charles Franklin Kettering, in *The International Encyclopedia of Thoughts,* page 315.
4. Dr. Raymond C. Ortlund, *The Best Half of Life* (Glendale, California: Gospel Light/Regal Books, 1979).